NORTHERN LIGHTS
KNIT

---

8 ICELANDIC
INSPIRED PROJECTS

CONTENTS

GERDA PULLOVER

◖■■□▭ **EASY**

SIZES

S{M, L, 1X, 2X}

Finished Bust:
About 39{43, 47, 51, 55}"/
99{109, 119.5, 129.5, 139.5} cm

Finished Length:
About 24½{25, 25½, 26, 26½}"/
62{63.5, 65, 66, 67.5} cm

Note: Pattern is written for smallest size
with changes for larger sizes in braces.
When only one number is given, it
applies to all sizes.
To follow pattern more easily, circle all
numbers pertaining to your size before
beginning.

GAUGE

16 sts and 22 rows = about 4" (10 cm)
in Texture pattern.

BE SURE TO CHECK YOUR GAUGE.

SHOPPING LIST
Yarn (Medium Weight)
LION BRAND® HEARTLAND®
(Art. #136)
- ☐ #126 Sequoia - 3{4, 4, 5, 5} balls (A)
- ☐ #125 Mammoth Cave -
  2{3, 3, 3, 4} balls (B)
- ☐ #109 Olympic -
  1{2, 2, 2, 2} ball(s) (C)

Knitting Needles
Circular, 24" (61 cm) long,
- ☐ Size 9 (5.5 mm)
  or size needed for gauge

Additional Supplies
- ☐ LION BRAND® stitch markers
- ☐ LION BRAND® stitch holders
- ☐ LION BRAND® large-eyed
  blunt needle

NOTES

1. Pullover is worked in 4 pieces: Back, Front, and 2 Sleeves.

2. The Back and Front are identical.

3. The Sleeves are designed using different colors on each Sleeve.

4. The neck edging is worked after all pieces are sewn together.

5. A circular needle is used for all pieces. When making Back, Front, and Sleeves, work back and forth in rows on the circular needle as if working on straight needles. The neck edging is worked in rounds.

6. When you see 'work even' in the instructions, this means to continue on in the pattern st you have established without changing the st count by increasing, decreasing, or binding off.

7. When you see 'as established' in the instructions, this means to continue in the current pattern st.

STITCH EXPLANATIONS

M1 (make 1)
An increase worked by lifting the horizontal strand lying between needles and placing it onto the left needle. Knit this new stitch through the back loop – one st increased.

ssk (slip, slip, knit)
Slip next 2 sts as if to knit, one at a time, to right needle; insert left needle into fronts of these 2 sts and knit them together – one st decreased.

PATTERN STITCH

Texture Pattern
(worked over an even number of sts)
Row 1 (RS): Knit.
Row 2: *K1, p1; rep from * to end of row.
Row 3: Knit.
Row 4: *P1, k1; rep from * to end of row.
Rep Rows 1-4 for Texture pattern.

BACK

With B, cast on 90{98, 106, 114, 122} sts.
With B, beg with Row 1 of pattern, work in Texture pattern for 10 rows.
Decrease Row (RS): With B, k1, k2tog, knit to last st, ssk, k1 – you will have 88{96, 104, 112, 120} sts in this row.
With B, beg with Row 4 of pattern, work in Texture pattern for 9 rows.
With B, rep Decrease Row – 86{94, 102, 110, 118} sts.

Rep last 10 rows for 4 more times, working Decrease Row every 10th row and changing yarn color as follows:
Work 1 more row with B, 16 rows with C, and 23 rows with A – 78{86, 94, 102, 110} sts when all decreases have been completed.
With A, continue even in Texture pattern as established until piece measures about 16" (40.5 cm) from beg, end with a WS row as the last row you work.

Shape Raglan Armholes

Row 1 (RS): With A, bind off 6{7, 8, 9, 10} sts, work in Texture pattern as established to end of row – 72{79, 86, 93, 100} sts.
Row 2: With A, bind off 6{7, 8, 9, 10} sts, work in Texture pattern as established to end of row – 66{72, 78, 84, 90} sts.

Row 3 (Decrease Row – RS): With A, k1, k2tog, knit to last 3 sts, ssk, k1 – 64{70, 76, 82, 88} sts.
Rows 4-6: With A, work even in Texture pattern as established.
Row 7: With A, rep Row 3 – 62{68, 74, 80, 86} sts.
Rep Rows 4-7 for 3{2, 2, 1, 0} more time(s) – 56{64, 70, 78, 86} sts when all decreases have been completed.

Next Row (WS): With A, work even in Texture pattern as established.
Next Row: With A, rep Row 3 – 54{62, 68, 76, 84} sts.
Next Row: With A, work even in Texture pattern as established.
Change to B.
Next Row (RS): With B, rep Row 3 – 52{60, 66, 74, 82} sts.
Next Row: With B, work even in Texture pattern as established.
Rep last 2 rows 11{15, 17, 20, 24} more times – 30{30, 32, 34, 34} sts rem when all decreases have been completed.
Place rem 30{30, 32, 34, 34} sts on a st holder.

FRONT

With B, cast on 90{98, 106, 114, 122} sts and make same as Back.

RIGHT SLEEVE

Stripe Sequence
With B, work 44 rows; with A, work to Shape Raglan; with A, work 10{8, 18, 22, 24} rows; with C, work 28{28, 16, 20, 28} rows; with B, work to end of Sleeve.
With B, cast on 50{52, 54, 56, 58} sts.

Begin Stripe Sequence and shape sleeve as follows:
Beg with Row 1 of pattern, work in Texture pattern for 22 rows.
Increase Row (RS): K1, M1, knit to last st, M1, k1 – 52{54, 56, 58, 60} sts.
Rep Increase Row every 14th{12th, 8th, 6th, 4th} row 3{4, 6, 9, 14} times more – 58{62, 68, 76, 88} sts when all increases have been completed.
Work even in Texture pattern as established until piece measures about 18" (45.5 cm) from beg, end with a WS row as the last row you work.

Note: When you see '0' repeats in an instruction, this means that you should not perform that particular instruction, just skip to the next part of the instruction.

Shape Raglan Armholes
Continue in Stripe Sequence as follows:
Row 1 (RS): Bind off 6{7, 8, 9, 10} sts, work in Texture pattern as established to end of row – 52{55, 60, 67, 78} sts.
Row 2: Bind off 6{7, 8, 9, 10} sts, work in Texture pattern as established to end of row – 46{48, 52, 58, 68} sts.
Row 3 (Decrease Row – RS): K1, k2tog, knit to last 3 sts, ssk, k1 – 44{46, 50, 56, 66} sts.
Rep Decrease Row every 4th row 10{11, 11, 9, 6} times, then every 2nd row 1{1, 3, 8, 16} time(s) – 24 sts when all decreases have been completed.
Purl 1 row.
Place rem 24 sts on a st holder.

LEFT SLEEVE
Stripe Sequence
With C, work 22 rows; with A, work to Shape Raglan; with B, work 16{20, 20, 24, 28} rows; with C, work to end of Sleeve.

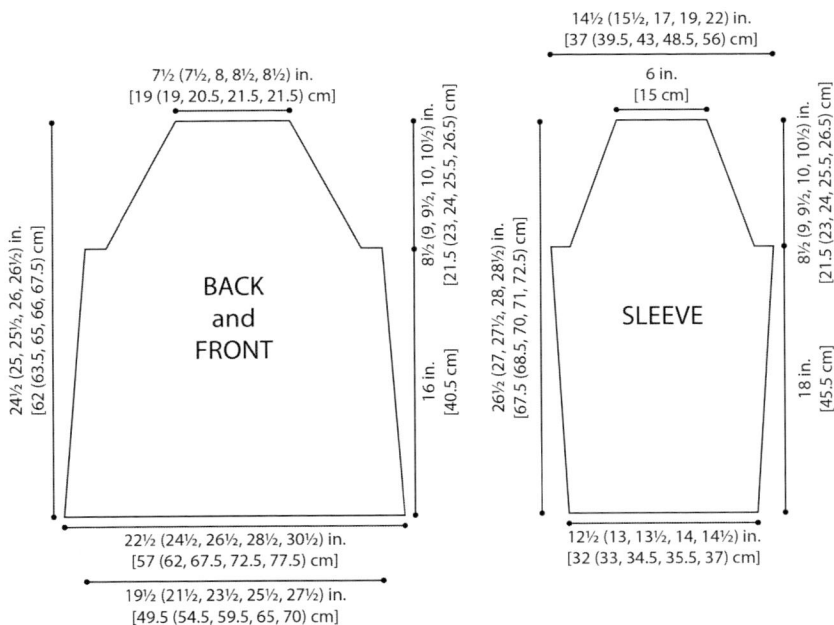

With C, cast on 50{52, 54, 56, 58} sts. Following Left Sleeve Stripe Sequence, work same as Right Sleeve.

FINISHING
Sew raglan edges of Sleeves to Front and Back raglan armholes.
Sew Sleeve seams.
Sew side seams, leaving 4" (10 cm) unsewn at lower edge for side slits.

Neck Edging
From RS, slip all sts from holders onto needle. Place marker for beg of rnd.
Rnds 1-6: With B, *k1, p1; rep from * around.
Bind off all sts.
Weave in ends.

7½ (7½, 8, 8½, 8½) in.
[19 (19, 20.5, 21.5, 21.5) cm]

24½ (25, 25½, 26, 26½) in.
[62 (63.5, 65, 66, 67.5) cm]

BACK and FRONT

8½ (9, 9½, 10, 10½) in.
[21.5 (23, 24, 25.5, 26.5) cm]

16 in.
[40.5 cm]

22½ (24½, 26½, 28½, 30½) in.
[57 (62, 67.5, 72.5, 77.5) cm]

19½ (21½, 23½, 25½, 27½) in.
[49.5 (54.5, 59.5, 65, 70) cm]

14½ (15½, 17, 19, 22) in.
[37 (39.5, 43, 48.5, 56) cm]

6 in.
[15 cm]

26½ (27, 27½, 28, 28½) in.
[67.5 (68.5, 70, 71, 72.5) cm]

SLEEVE

8½ (9, 9½, 10, 10½) in.
[21.5 (23, 24, 25.5, 26.5) cm]

18 in.
[45.5 cm]

12½ (13, 13½, 14, 14½) in.
[32 (33, 34.5, 35.5, 37) cm]

BIRGER CARDIGAN

■■■□▭ **EASY**

SIZES

XS/S{M/L, 1X/2X}

Finished Bust:
44{52, 60}"/112{132, 152.5} cm,
with Fronts overlapped

Finished Length:
23{24, 25}"/58.5{61, 63.5} cm

Note: Pattern is written for smallest size with changes for larger sizes in braces. When only one number is given, it applies to all sizes.
To follow pattern more easily, circle all numbers pertaining to your size before beginning.

GAUGE

13 sts = about 5½" (14 cm);
13 rows = about 4½" (11.5 cm) in St st (knit on RS, purl on WS).

BE SURE TO CHECK YOUR GAUGE.

SHOPPING LIST

SUPER BULKY (6)

Yarn (Super Bulky Weight)
LION BRAND® HOMETOWN USA®
(Art. #135)
☐ #218 Bar Harbor Blizzard -
   7{9, 11} balls (A)
☐ #150 Chicago Charcoal -
   3{4, 5} balls (B)

Knitting Needles
LION BRAND® circular knitting needle, 29" (73.5 cm) long,
☐ Size 11 (8 mm)
   or size needed for gauge

Additional Supplies
☐ LION BRAND® stitch markers
☐ LION BRAND® large-eyed blunt needle

NOTES

1. Cardigan is worked in 5 pieces: Back, 2 Fronts, and 2 Sleeves.

2. Each piece is worked in St st (knit on RS, purl on WS) with 2 colors of yarn.

3. The Front bands are worked in Garter st (knit every st on every row) in one with each Front.

4. Simple embroidery is worked onto each completed piece.

5. Cardigan is designed without a neck band.

6. A circular needle is used to accommodate the number of sts. Work back and forth in rows on the circular needle as if working on straight needles.

STITCH EXPLANATION
M1 (make 1)
An increase worked by lifting the horizontal strand lying between needles and placing it onto the left needle. Knit this new stitch through the back loop – one st increased.

STRIPE SEQUENCE
Row 1 (RS): With B, knit.
Rows 2-6: With B, continue in St st.
Rows 7-16: With A, work in St st.
Repeat Rows 1-16 for Stripe Sequence.

BACK
With A, cast on 52{62, 71} sts.

Edging Row (WS): Knit.

Beg with a RS row, work in St st (knit on RS, purl on WS) with A for 6 rows (thus ending with a WS row).

Beginning with Row 1, work in Stripe Sequence until piece measures about 21½{22½, 23½}"/54.5{57, 59.5} cm from beg, end with a Row 6, 8, 10, 12, 14 or 16 of Stripe Sequence as the last row you work.

The last row you worked will have been a WS (purl) row.

Change to A, and continue with A only for the remainder of the Back.

Shape Shoulders
Row 1 (RS): Bind off 6{8, 10} sts, knit to end of row – 46{54, 61} sts.
Row 2: Bind off 6{8, 10} sts, purl to end of row – 40{46, 51} sts.

For Neck Shaping and to continue Shaping Shoulders, place a marker on each side of center 12{14, 15} sts.

Row 3 (RS): Bind off 7{8, 9} sts, knit to next marker for right shoulder; join a 2nd ball of yarn and bind off center 12{14, 15} sts, knit to end of row for left shoulder – 7{8, 9} sts for right shoulder and 14{16, 18} sts for left shoulder.

You'll now work both shoulders AT THE SAME TIME with separate balls of yarn.

Row 4: On left shoulder, bind off 7{8, 9} sts, purl to end of side; on right shoulder, purl to end of side – 7{8, 9} sts for each shoulder.
Row 5: On right shoulder, bind off rem 7{8, 9} sts; on left shoulder, knit to end of side.
Bind off rem 7{8, 9}sts of left shoulder.

LEFT FRONT
With A, cast on 33{38, 43} sts.

Edging Row (WS): Knit.

Row 1 (RS): Knit.
Row 2: K3 for front band, purl to end of row.
Rows 3-6: Repeat Rows 1 and 2 twice.

Keeping 3 front band sts in Garter st (knit every st on every row) and beginning with Row 1 of sequence, work in Stripe Sequence until piece measures about 18{19, 20}"/45.5{48.5, 51} cm from beg, end with any RS row of Stripe Sequence except Row 7 or 9 as the last row you work.

Note: It is important to end with a specific RS row here to ensure that the Stripe Sequence continues to flow smoothly through the shaping that follows.

Shape Neck
As you shape the neck, continue in Stripe Sequence as established.
Row 1 (WS): Bind off 7{8, 8} sts, purl to end row – 26{30, 35} sts.
Rows 2, 4 and 6: Knit.
Row 3: Bind off 3{3, 4} sts, purl to end of row – 23{27, 31} sts.
Row 5: Bind off 2 sts, purl to end of row – 21{25, 29} sts.
Row 7: Bind off one st, purl to end of row – 20{24, 28} sts.
Rows 8-11: Work even in St st.

Change to A, and continue with A only for the remainder of the Left Front.

Shape Shoulder
Row 12 (RS): Bind off 6{8, 10} sts, knit to end of row – 14{16, 18} sts.
Rows 13 and 15: Purl.
Row 14: Bind off 7{8, 9}sts, knit to end of row – 7{8, 9} sts.
Bind off rem 7{8, 9} sts.

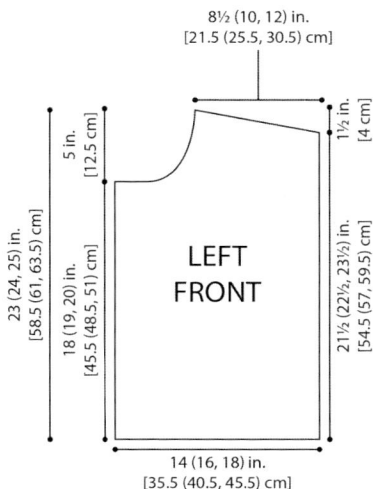

RIGHT FRONT
With A, cast on 33{38, 43} sts.

Edging Row (WS): Knit.
Row 1 (RS): Knit.
Row 2: Purl to last 3 sts, k3 for front band.
Rows 3-6: Repeat Rows 1 and 2.

Keeping 3 front band sts in Garter st and beginning with Row 1 of sequence, work in Stripe Sequence until piece measures same as Left Front to Neck Shaping, end with any WS row of Stripe Sequence except Row 6, 8 or 10 as the last row you work.

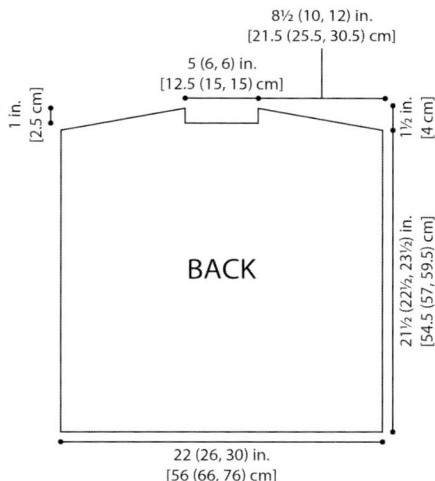

Shape Neck
As you shape the neck, continue in Stripe Sequence as established.
Row 1 (RS): Bind off 7{8, 8} sts, knit to end of row – 26{30, 35} sts.
Rows 2, 4 and 6: Purl.
Row 3: Bind off 3{3, 4} sts, knit to end of row – 23{27, 31} sts.
Row 5: Bind off 2 sts, knit to end of row – 21{25, 29} sts.
Row 7: Bind off one st, knit to end of row – 20{24, 28} sts.
Rows 8-11: Work even in St st.

Change to A, and continue with A only for the remainder of the Right Front.

Shape Shoulder
Row 12 (WS): Bind off 6{8, 10} sts, purl to end of row – 14{16, 18} sts.
Rows 13 and 15: Knit.
Row 14: Bind off 7{8, 9} sts, purl to end of row – 7{8, 9} sts.
Bind off rem 7 (8, 9) sts.

BACK

8½ (10, 12) in.
[21.5 (25.5, 30.5) cm]

5 (6, 6) in.
[12.5 (15, 15) cm]

1 in.
[2.5 cm]

1½ in.
[4 cm]

21½ (22½, 23½) in.
[54.5 (57, 59.5) cm]

22 (26, 30) in.
[56 (66, 76) cm]

LEFT FRONT

8½ (10, 12) in.
[21.5 (25.5, 30.5) cm]

5 in.
[12.5 cm]

1½ in.
[4 cm]

23 (24, 25) in.
[58.5 (61, 63.5) cm]

18 (19, 20) in.
[45.5 (48.5, 51) cm]

21½ (22½, 23½) in.
[54.5 (57, 59.5) cm]

14 (16, 18) in.
[35.5 (40.5, 45.5) cm]

SLEEVES (MAKE 2)

With A, cast on 19{21, 24} sts.

Edging Row (WS): Knit.

Row 1 (Increase Row – RS): With A, k1, M1, k to last st, M1, k1 – 21 (23, 26) sts.
Rows 2-6: With A, work in St st.

Beginning with Row 1 of sequence, work in Stripe Sequence AND AT THE SAME TIME shape Sleeve as follows:
Row 7: Repeat Increase Row – 23{25, 28} sts.
Rows 8-12: Work in St st.

Row 13: Repeat Increase Row – 25{27, 30} sts.
Rows 14-16: Work in St st.
Row 17: Repeat Increase Row – 27{29, 32} sts.
Rows 18-20: Work in St st.
Row 21: Repeat Increase Row – 29{31, 35} sts.
Row 22: Work in St st.

Rep Rows 7-22, then rep Rows 7-12{16, 20} once more – 39{43, 48} sts when all increases have been completed.

Continue in St st and Stripe Sequence and work until piece measures about 19" (48.5 cm) from beg, end with a Row 6, 8, 10, 12, 14 or 16 of Stripe Sequence as the last row you work.

Shape Sleeve Cap

Change to A, and continue with A only for the remainder of the Sleeve.

Row 1 (RS): Bind off 7{8, 9} sts, knit to end of row – 32{35, 39} sts.
Row 2: Bind off 7 {8, 9} sts, purl to end of row – 25{27, 30} sts.
Rows 3 and 4: Rep Rows 1 and 2 – 11{11, 12} sts. Bind off rem 11{11, 12} sts.

FINISHING
Embroidery

With A, embroider 2 lines of straight sts along every B-colored stripe. On our sample, we spaced our straight sts over and under 2 St sts.

Sew shoulder seams.

Place markers on side edges of Back and Fronts, about 8{9, 10}"/20.5{23, 25.5} cm below shoulder seams.
Sew tops of Sleeves between markers.
Sew side and Sleeve seams.

Weave in ends.

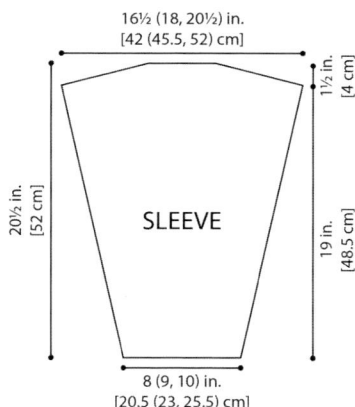

16½ (18, 20½) in.
[42 (45.5, 52) cm]

1½ in.
[4 cm]

20½ in.
[52 cm]

SLEEVE

19 in.
[48.5 cm]

8 (9, 10) in.
[20.5 (23, 25.5) cm]

HULDRA HAT

◖■■□▷ EASY

SIZE

Finished Circumference:
About 19" (48.5 cm), will stretch to fit
a range of sizes

GAUGE

18 sts = about 4" (10 cm) in St st worked in
rnds (knit every st on every rnd).

BE SURE TO CHECK YOUR GAUGE.

SHOPPING LIST

Yarn (Bulky Weight)
LION BRAND® SCARFIE®
(Art. #826)
☐ #201 Cream/Black - 1 ball

Knitting Needles
LION BRAND® double-pointed
knitting needles (set of 5), and
circular, 16" (40.5 cm) long,
☐ Size 8 (5 mm)
   or size needed for gauge

Additional Supplies
☐ LION BRAND® stitch markers
☐ LION BRAND® large-eyed
   blunt needle
☐ 3" x 3" (7.5 cm x 7.5 cm) piece
   of cardboard

NOTES

1. Earflaps are worked first, then stitches are cast on between Earflaps for the back of Hat.

2. Lower back of Hat is worked in rows then stitches are cast on for front of Hat and work is joined to work in the round.

3. Decreases are worked to shape top of Hat. When stitches have been sufficiently decreased, double pointed needles are used instead of the circular needle.

4. Stitches are picked up on lower edge of each Earflap for the cords.

5. Tassels are tied to the end of each cord and to the top of the Hat.

STITCH EXPLANATIONS

M1 (make 1)
An increase worked by lifting the horizontal strand lying between needles and placing it onto the left needle. Knit this new stitch through the back loop – one st increased.

ssk (slip, slip, knit)
Slip next 2 sts as if to knit, one at a time, to right needle; insert left needle into fronts of these 2 sts and knit them tog – one st decreased.

TECHNIQUE EXPLANATION

Cable Cast On
*Insert right needle between first 2 sts on left needle, wrap yarn and pull through (as if knitting a st), transfer new st to left needle; rep from * for desired number of sts.

FIRST EARFLAP
With double-pointed needle (dpn), cast on 4 sts. Work back and forth in rows using 2 dpns.

Row 1 (WS): Purl.
Row 2 (Increase Row): K1, M1, knit to last st, M1, k1 – 6 sts.
Rows 3-14: Rep Rows 1 and 2 for 6 more times – you will have 18 sts in Row 14.
Row 15: Purl.
Cut yarn, leaving sts on one dpn, and set aside.

SECOND EARFLAP
Cast on and make same as First Earflap, but do not cut yarn.

Cast On for Back of Hat
From RS, with circular needle and yarn still attached to Second Earflap, knit across sts of Second Earflap; turn, cable cast on 21 sts for back of Hat, turn; with same yarn, knit across sts of First Earflap – you will have 57 sts.

Next Row (WS): K17, k2tog, k19, k2tog, knit to end of row – 55 sts.
Beg with a RS (knit) row, work in St st (knit on RS, purl on WS) for 4 rows.

Cast On for Front of Hat and Join
Next Rnd (RS): Cable cast on 30 sts for front of Hat; beg over sts just cast on, k29, k2tog, k16, k2tog, k17, k2tog, knit to last st, being careful not to twist sts, knit the last st together with the first cast on st – 81 sts. Place marker for beg of rnd.

Work in St st worked in rnds (knit every st on every rnd) until Hat measures about 8½" (21.5 cm) measured from cast-on sts at front.

Shape Top of Hat
Note: Change from circular needle to double-pointed needles when sts have been sufficiently decreased.

Rnd 1: *K25, k2tog; rep from * 2 more times – 78 sts.
Rnd 2: Knit.
Rnd 3 (Decrease Rnd): (K11, k2tog) 6 times – 72 sts.
Rnd 4: Knit.
Rnd 5 (Decrease Rnd): (K10, k2tog) 6 times – 66 sts.
Rnd 6 (Decrease Rnd): (K9, k2tog) 6 times – 60 sts.
Rnd 7 (Decrease Rnd): (K8, k2tog) 6 times – 54 sts.
Rnd 8 (Decrease Rnd): (K7, k2tog) 6 times – 48 sts.
Rnd 9 (Decrease Rnd): (K6, k2tog) 6 times – 42 sts.
Rnd 10 (Decrease Rnd): (K5, k2tog) 6 times – 36 sts.
Rnd 11 (Decrease Rnd): (K4, k2tog) 6 times – 30 sts.
Rnd 12 (Decrease Rnd): (K3, k2tog) 6 times – 24 sts.
Rnd 13 (Decrease Rnd): (K2, k2tog) 6 times – 18 sts.
Rnd 14 (Decrease Rnd): (K1, k2tog) 6 times – 12 sts.
Rnd 15 (Decrease Rnd): K2tog around – 6 sts.
Cut yarn, leaving a long yarn tail. Thread yarn tail into blunt needle, then draw through rem sts. Pull tail to close opening at top of Hat. Knot securely.

FINISHING
Cords
From RS with dpn, pick up and k4 sts evenly spaced across cast-on edge of First Earflap.

Knit the 4 sts. Do not turn work. *Slide sts to other end of needle and knit them, pulling yarn tightly across the back of the work, (do not turn work); rep from * until cord measures about 4½" (11.5 cm) or desired length.

Last Row: (K2tog) twice.
Cut yarn, leaving a long yarn tail. Thread yarn tail into blunt needle, then draw through rem 2 sts. Knot securely.
Rep to make a cord on Second Earflap.

TASSELS (MAKE 3)
Wrap yarn around 3" (7.5 cm) cardboard about 23 times. Cut a 12" (30.5 cm) length of yarn and thread, doubled, into large-eyed blunt needle. Insert needle under all strands at upper edge of cardboard. Pull tightly and knot securely near strands. Cut yarn loops at lower edge of cardboard. Cut a 10" (25.5 cm) length of yarn and wrap tightly around loops about ¾" (2 cm) below top knot to form tassel neck. Knot securely; thread ends onto needle and weave ends to center of tassel.
Trim tassel ends evenly.

Tie a tassel to the end of each cord and to top of Hat.

Weave in ends.

JOOST PANTS

■■□□ **EASY**

SIZE

S{M, L, 1X, 2X}

Finished Waist:
About 28{32, 36, 40, 44}"/
71{81.5, 91.5, 101.5, 112} cm, can be
adjusted with the drawstring

Finished Hip:
About 36{40, 44, 48, 52}"/
91.5{101.5, 112, 122, 132} cm

Finished Inseam: About
26½"(67.5 cm) or to desired length

Note: Pattern is written for smallest size
with changes for larger sizes in braces.
When only one number is given, it
applies to all sizes.
To follow pattern more easily, circle all
numbers pertaining to your size before
beginning.

GAUGE

With larger size needles, 18 sts = about 4"
(10 cm) in St st worked in rnds (knit every
st on every rnd).

BE SURE TO CHECK YOUR GAUGE.

SHOPPING LIST

Yarn (Medium Weight) **4**
LION BRAND® JEANS® (Art. #505)
☐ #150 Vintage - 5{6, 7, 8, 8} balls

Knitting Needles
LION BRAND® double-pointed
knitting needles (set of 5),
☐ Size 5 (3.75 mm) and
☐ Size 8 (5 mm)
Circular, 16" (40.5 cm) long,
☐ Size 8 (5 mm)
Sizes S and M ONLY
Circular, 24" (61 cm) long,
☐ Size 5 (3.75 mm) **and**
☐ Size 8 (5 mm)
Sizes L, 1X and 2X ONLY
Circular, 32" (81.5 cm) long,
☐ Size 5 (3.75 mm) **and**
☐ Size 8 (5 mm)
Circular, 40" (101.5 cm) long,
☐ Size 8 (5 mm)
    or sizes needed for gauge

Additional Supplies
☐ LION BRAND® stitch markers
☐ LION BRAND® stitch holders
☐ LION BRAND® large-eyed
    blunt needle

NOTES

1. Pants are worked in one piece in the round from the top downwards.

2. The waist edge is folded and seamed to make a casing for the drawstring.

3. Below waist shaping is worked with short rows. Short rows are rows that are worked over
a portion of the sts in a row, leaving the remaining sts unworked. To work short rows, the
pattern instructions will tell you to 'turn' before you reach the end of the row.

4. At crotch, piece is divided, then legs are worked separately to ankle.

5. When you see 'work even' in the instructions, this means to continue on in the current
pattern st without changing the st count by increasing, decreasing, or binding off.

STITCH EXPLANATIONS

M1L (make 1 – left slanting)
An increase worked by lifting the horizontal strand lying between needles from front to back and placing it onto the left needle. Knit this new stitch through the back loop – 1 st increased.

M1R (make 1 – right slanting)
An increase worked by lifting the horizontal strand lying between needles from back to front and placing it onto the left needle. Knit this new stitch through the front loop – one st increased.

ssk (slip, slip, knit)
Slip next 2 sts as if to knit, one at a time, to right needle; insert left needle into fronts of these 2 sts and knit them together – one st decreased.

yo (yarn over)
An increase that also creates a small decorative hole (eyelet) in the fabric, worked as follows:
1. Bring yarn to front, between the needles.
2. Take yarn to back, over the right needle. This creates the new st. You are now ready to proceed with the next st as instructed.

PATTERN STITCH

K1, P1 Rib worked in rnds
(worked over an even number of sts)
Rnd 1 (RS): *K1, p1; rep from * to end of rnd.
Rnd 2: Knit the knit sts and purl the purl sts.
Rep Rnd 2 for K1, P1 Rib worked in rnds.

TECHNIQUE EXPLANATIONS

w&t (wrap and turn)
A technique used to ensure that a small hole doesn't form at the end of a short row.
1. Bring yarn between needles to front. Take care not to wrap the yarn over a needle, this would create a new st.
2. Slip next st as if to purl.
3. Bring yarn between needles to back. This will place a wrap around the st.
4. Slip same st back to left needle.
5. Turn work and bring yarn in position for next st.
6. The next time you knit this st on a RS row, pick up the wrap and knit it together with the st.

Cable Cast On
Make a slip knot on left needle, knit one st through slip knot, but do not drop slip knot from left needle, transfer new st from right needle to left needle – 2 sts on left needle. *Insert right needle between first 2 sts on left needle, wrap yarn and pull through (as if knitting a st), transfer new st to left needle; rep from * for desired number of sts.

PANTS

Waistband Ribbing
For sizes S and M, use the smaller 24" (61 cm) needle; for sizes L, 1X and 2X, use the smaller 32" (81.5 cm) needle.

With smaller size circular needle, cast on 126{144, 162, 180, 198} sts.
Place marker for beg of rnd. Join by working the first st on left hand needle with the working yarn from the right hand needle and being careful not to twist sts.

Work in K1, P1 Rib until piece measures about 4" (10 cm) from beg.
Next Rnd (Eyelet Rnd): K1, p1, k1, yo, k2tog; continue in K1, P1 Rib to last 6 sts, ssk, yo, (k1, p1) twice.
Continue in K1, P1 Rib until piece measures about 5" (12.5 cm) from beg.

Short Row Shaping
For sizes S and M, use the larger 24" (61 cm) needle; for sizes L, 1X and 2X, use the larger 40" (101.5 cm) needle.

Change to larger size circular needle.
Row 1: Knit to last 16{19, 21, 23, 25} sts, w&t, purl to last 16{19, 21, 23, 25} sts, w&t.
Rows 2-6: Knit to 9{10, 11, 12, 13} sts before the wrapped st of previous row, w&t, purl to 9{10, 11, 12, 13} sts before the wrapped st of previous row, w&t.

Next Rnd: Knit to beg of rnd marker, picking up each wrap and knitting it together with the wrapped st.
Next Rnd: Rep last rnd.

Work even in St st worked in the rnd (knit every st on every rnd) for 10 rnds.
Next Rnd: K63{72, 81, 90, 99}, place marker (pm) for center back, knit to end of rnd.

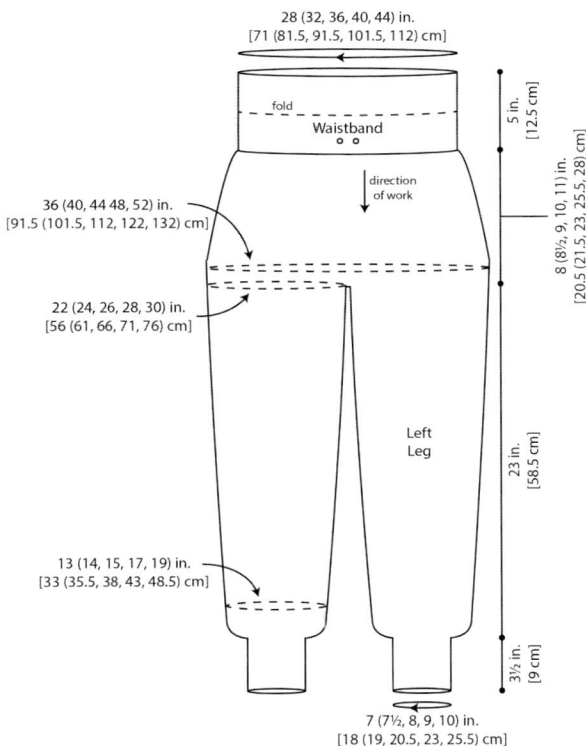

28 (32, 36, 40, 44) in.
[71 (81.5, 91.5, 101.5, 112) cm]

fold

Waistband

direction
of work

5 in.
[12.5 cm]

8 (8½, 9, 10, 11) in.
[20.5 (21.5, 23, 25.5, 28) cm]

36 (40, 44 48, 52) in.
[91.5 (101.5, 112, 122, 132) cm]

22 (24, 26, 28, 30) in.
[56 (61, 66, 71, 76) cm]

Left
Leg

23 in.
[58.5 cm]

13 (14, 15, 17, 19) in.
[33 (35.5, 38, 43, 48.5) cm]

3½ in.
[9 cm]

7 (7½, 8, 9, 10) in.
[18 (19, 20.5, 23, 25.5) cm]

Next Rnd (Increase Rnd): *K1, M1R, knit to one st before marker, M1L, k1, slip marker (sm); rep from * to end of rnd – you will have 130{148, 166, 184, 202} sts in this rnd. Work even in St st for 3{3, 3, 5, 5} rnds. Rep Increase Rnd – 134{152, 170, 188, 206} sts. Rep last 4{4, 4, 6, 6} rnds 4{5, 7, 2, 5} more times – 150{172, 198, 196, 226} sts when all increases have been completed.

Sizes S (M, 1X, 2X) ONLY

Knit 1{1, 3, 3} rnd(s).
Rep Increase Rnd – 154{176, 200, 230} sts.
Rep last 2 {2, 4, 4} rnds 2{1, 4, 1} more time(s) – 162{180, 216, 234} sts when all increases have been completed.

All Sizes

Remove beg of rnd marker and center back marker.

Divide for Legs

Place last 81{90, 99, 108, 117} sts worked onto large stitch holder or spare needle for right leg.

LEFT LEG

You will now be working back and forth in rows on the 81{90, 99, 108, 117} left leg sts only.

Shape Crotch

Row 1 (RS): Using Cable Cast On, cast on one st, knit to end of row – 82{91, 100, 109, 118} sts.
Row 2: Using Cable Cast On, cast on 2 sts, purl to end of row – 84{93, 102, 111, 120} sts.
Row 3: Using Cable Cast On, cast on 2 sts, knit to end of row – 86{95, 104, 113, 122} sts.
Rows 4 and 5: Rep Rows 2 and 3 – 90{99, 108, 117, 126} sts.
Row 6: Using Cable Cast On, cast on 3 sts at beg of row, purl to end of row – 93{102, 111, 120, 129} sts.
Row 7: Rep Row 3 – 95 {104, 113, 122, 131} sts.
Row 8: Using Cable Cast On, cast on 4 sts, purl to end of row – 99{108, 117, 126, 135} sts.

Shape Leg
Next Row/Rnd (RS): Knit.
You will now return to working in rnds. Place marker for beg of rnd. Join by working the first st on left hand needle with the working yarn from the right hand needle and being careful not to twist sts.

Note: As sts are sufficiently decreased, change to shorter large size circular needle and then to large size dpn.

Knit one rnd.
Next Rnd (Decrease Rnd): K1, ssk, knit to last 3 sts, k2tog, k1 – 97{106, 115, 124, 133} sts. Rep last 2 rnds 3 more times – 91{100, 109, 118, 127} sts when all decreases have been completed.

Knit 3 rnds.
Rep Decrease Rnd – 89{98, 107, 116, 125} sts. Rep last 4 rnds one more time – 87{96, 105, 114, 123} sts.

Knit 7{5, 5, 5, 5} rnds.
Rep Decrease Rnd – 85{94, 103, 112, 121} sts. Rep last 8{6, 6, 6, 6} rnds 7{6, 14, 14, 14} more times – 71{82, 75, 84, 93} sts when all decreases have been completed.

Knit 9 {7, 7, 7, 7} rnds.
Rep Decrease Rnd – 69{80, 73, 82, 91} sts. Rep last 10{8, 8, 8, 8} rnds 5{9, 3, 3, 3} more times – 59{62, 67, 76, 85} sts when all decreases have been completed.

Work even in St st until leg measures about 23" (58.5 cm) from crotch.

Notes: If extra length is needed, carefully try on pants to determine desired length. Length should be total leg length minus 3½" (9 cm).
Work even in St st to desired length minus 3½" (9 cm).

Cuff
Next Rnd (Decrease Rnd): *K2, k2tog; rep from * to last 3{2, 3, 8, 5} sts, k1{0, 1, 2, 2}, k2tog, knit to end of rnd – 44{46, 50, 58, 64} sts.

Change to smaller size dpn.
Work in K1, P1 Rib for about 3½" (9 cm). Bind off loosely.

RIGHT LEG
Return 81{90, 99, 108, 117} sts of right leg to long larger circular needle, so that you are ready to work a RS row.

Shape Crotch
Row 1 (RS): Using Cable Cast On, cast on 2 sts, knit to end of row – 83{92, 101, 110, 119} sts.
Row 2: Using Cable Cast On, cast on one st, purl to end of row – 84{93, 102, 111, 120} sts.
Row 3: Using Cable Cast On, cast on 2 sts, knit to end of row – 86{95, 104, 113, 122} sts.
Row 4: Using Cable Cast On, cast on 2 sts, purl to end of row – 88{97, 106, 115, 124} sts.
Row 5: Using Cable Cast On, cast on 3 sts, knit to end of row – 91 {100, 109, 118, 127} sts.
Row 6: Rep Row 4 – 93{102, 111, 120, 129} sts
Row 7: Using Cable Cast On, cast on 4 sts at beg of row, knit to end of row – 97{106, 115, 124, 133} sts.
Row 8: Rep Row 4 – 99{108, 117, 126, 135} sts.

Shape Leg
Work same as Left Leg shaping to end.

FINISHING
Sew crotch seam.
Fold waistband ribbing to inside and sew edge in place to form waistband casing.

Drawstring
With 2 small dpn, cast on 3 sts. Knit the 3 sts. Do not turn work. *Slide sts to other end of needle and knit them, pulling yarn tightly across the back of the work, (do not turn work); rep from * until drawstring measures about 62{66, 70, 74, 78}/157.5{167.5, 178, 188, 198} cm long. Bind off all sts.
Thread drawstring through waistband casing, taking ends of cord to RS through eyelets.

Weave in ends.

BETANIA CARDIGAN

◖■■☐☐▷ **EASY**

SIZE

X/S{M/L, 1X/2X}
Finished Bust: 40{49, 58}"/
101.5{124.5, 147.5} cm
Finished Length: 32{34, 36}"/
81.5{86.5, 91.5} cm

Note: Pattern is written for smallest size with changes for larger sizes in parentheses. When only one number is given, it applies to all sizes. To follow pattern more easily, circle all numbers pertaining to your size before beginning.

GAUGE

With larger size needles,
9 sts and 12 rows = about 4" (10 cm)
in St st (knit on RS, purl on WS).

BE SURE TO CHECK YOUR GAUGE.

SHOPPING LIST

SUPER BULKY 6

Yarn (Super Bulky Weight)
LION BRAND® WOOL-EASE®
THICK & QUICK® (Art. #640)
- ☐ #149 Charcoal - 5{6, 7} balls (A)
- ☐ #612 Coney Island - 4{5, 6} balls (B)
- ☐ #609 Moonlight - 2{3, 3} balls (C)
- ☐ #535 River Run - 3{3, 4} balls (D)
- ☐ #154 Grey Marble - 1{2, 2} ball(s) (E)

Knitting Needles
Circular, 40" (101.5 cm) long,
- ☐ Size 11 (8 mm) **and**
Circular, 32" (81.5 cm) long,
- ☐ Size 13 (9 mm)
  or sizes needed for gauge

Additional Supplies
- ☐ LION BRAND® stitch markers
- ☐ LION BRAND® stitch holders
- ☐ LION BRAND® large-eyed blunt needle

NOTES

1. Cardigan is worked in 5 pieces: Back, Left Front, Right Front, and 2 Sleeves.

2. Yarn colors are changed to make stripes.

3. Stitches for the front bands and collar are picked up along front edge of the Cardigan.

4. Front bands and collar are shaped by working short rows. Short rows are rows that are worked over a portion of the sts in a row, leaving the remaining sts unworked. To work short rows, the pattern instructions will tell you to 'turn' before you reach the end of the row.

5. A circular needle is used to accommodate the number of sts. Work back and forth with the circular needle as if working on straight needles.

6. When you see 'as established' in the instructions, this means to continue in the current pattern st. For example, to continue in a rib pattern, knit the knit sts and purl the purl sts.

STITCH EXPLANATIONS

M1 (make 1)

An increase worked by lifting the horizontal strand lying between needles and placing it onto the left needle. Knit this new stitch through the back loop – one st increased.

ssk (slip, slip, knit)

Slip next 2 sts as if to knit, one at a time, to right needle; insert left needle into fronts of these 2 sts and knit them together – one st decreased.

PATTERN STITCH

K1, P1 Rib

(worked over an odd number of sts)
Row 1: K1, *p1, k1; rep from * to end of row.
Row 2: Knit the knit sts and purl the purl sts.
Rep Row 2 for K1, P1 Rib.

STRIPE SEQUENCE

*Work 12 rows with A, 14 rows with B, 8 rows with C, 10 rows with D, 6 rows with E; rep from * for Stripe Sequence.

BACK

Lower Ribbing

With smaller size needle and A, cast on 55{65, 75} sts.
Row 1 (RS): With A, work Row 1 of K1, P1 Rib.
Rows 2-12: Continue in K1, P1 Rib changing color following Stripe Sequence.

Body

Change to larger size needle.
Changing color following Stripe Sequence, work in St st (knit on RS, purl on WS) until piece measures about 4" (10 cm) above rib, end with a WS row as the last row you work.

* Decrease Row (RS): K1, k2tog, knit to last 3 sts, ssk, k1 – 53{63, 73} sts.
Continue in St st, changing color following Stripe Sequence, for 4" (10 cm), end with a WS row as the last row you work.

Rep from * 3 more times – 47{57, 67} sts.
Rep Decrease Row – 45{55, 65} sts.
Continue in St st, changing color following Stripe Sequence, until piece measures about 32{34, 36}"/81.5{86.5, 91.5} cm from beg.
Bind off.

POCKET LININGS (MAKE 2)

With larger size needle and D, cast on 17 sts.
Work in St st until piece measures about 9{10, 11}"/23{25.5, 28} cm from beg, end with a WS row as the last row you work.
Place these sts on a st holder.

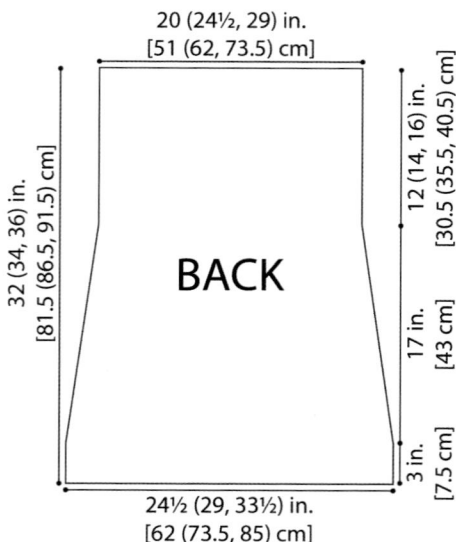

20 (24½, 29) in.
[51 (62, 73.5) cm]

32 (34, 36) in.
[81.5 (86.5, 91.5) cm]

12 (14, 16) in.
[30.5 (35.5, 40.5) cm]

BACK

17 in.
[43 cm]

3 in.
[7.5 cm]

24½ (29, 33½) in.
[62 (73.5, 85) cm]

LEFT FRONT

Lower Ribbing
With smaller size needle and A, cast on
25{29, 33} sts.
Row 1 (RS): With A, work Row 1 of K1, P1 Rib.
Rows 2-12: Continue in K1, P1 Rib
changing color following Stripe Sequence.

Body
Change to larger size needle.
Continue to change color following Stripe
Sequence.
Row 1 (RS): K5{7, 9}, place marker (pm),
work in K1, P1 Rib as established over next
17 sts, pm, k3{5, 7}.
Row 2: Purl to marker, slip marker (sm),
work in K1, P1 Rib to next marker, sm, purl
to end of row.
Row 3: Knit to marker, sm, work in K1, P1
Rib to next marker, sm, knit to end of row.
Row 4: Purl to marker, sm, work in K1, P1
Rib to next marker, sm, purl to end of row.
Rows 5-14: Rep last 2 rows 5 more times.
Row 15 (Decrease Row): K1, k2tog, knit to
marker, sm, work in K1, P1 Rib to next marker,
sm, knit to end of row – 24{28, 32} sts.
Rows 16-29: Rep Rows 2-15 – 23{27,
31} sts at the end of Row 29.
Rows 30 thru 31{33, 35}: Rep Rows 2
and 3 for 1{2, 3} time(s).

Join Pocket Lining
Remove markers while working next row.
Row 32{34, 36}: Purl to marker, bind off
17 sts between markers, purl to end of row.
Row 33{35, 37}: Knit to bound-off sts;
from RS, knit across sts of one Pocket
Lining from st holder, knit to end of row.
Rows 34{36, 38} thru 42: Work in St st
for 9{7, 5} rows.
Row 43 (Decrease Row): K1, k2tog, knit
to end of row – 22{26, 30} sts.
Rows 44 thru 48{54, 56}: Work in St st
for 5{11, 13} rows.

Size XS/S ONLY
Shape Neck
Row 49: Knit to last 3 sts, ssk, k1 – 21 sts.
Work in St st for 7 rows.
Row 57: Rep Row 43 – 20 sts.
Row 58: Purl.
Row 59: Rep Row 49 – 19 sts.
Work in St st for 9 rows.
Row 69: Rep Row 49 – 18 sts.

Row 70: Purl.
Row 71: Rep Row 43 – 17 sts.

Size M/L ONLY
Shape Neck
Row 55: Knit to last 3 sts, ssk, k1 – 25 sts.
Row 56: Purl.
Row 57: Rep Row 43 – 24 sts.
Work in St st for 7 rows.
Row 65: Rep Row 55 – 23 sts.
Work in St st for 5 rows.
Row 71: Rep Row 43 – 22 sts.

Size 1X/2X ONLY
Row 57: Rep Row 43 – 29 sts.
Work in St st for 3 rows.
Shape Neck
Row 61 (RS): Knit to last 3 sts, ssk, k1 –
28 sts.
Work in St st for 9 rows.
Row 71: K1, k2tog, knit to last 3 sts, ssk, k1 –
26 sts.

All Sizes
Work in St st for 7{3, 9} rows.
Row 79{75, 81}: Knit to last 3 sts, ssk, k1 –
16{21, 25} sts.
Work in St st for 9 rows.

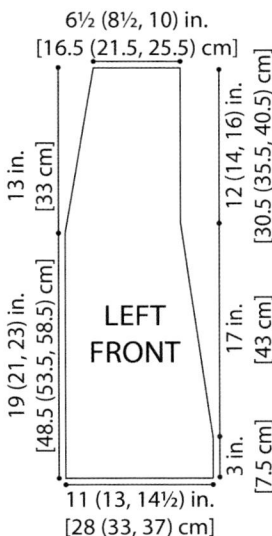

6½ (8½, 10) in.
[16.5 (21.5, 25.5) cm]

13 in.
[33 cm]

12 (14, 16) in.
[30.5 (35.5, 40.5) cm]

LEFT
FRONT

19 (21, 23) in.
[48.5 (53.5, 58.5) cm]

17 in.
[43 cm]

3 in.
[7.5 cm]

11 (13, 14½) in.
[28 (33, 37) cm]

Row 89{85, 91}: Knit to last 3 sts, ssk, k1 –
15{20, 24} sts.
Rep last 10 rows 0{1, 1} more time(s) –
15{19, 23} sts.

Work even in St st until piece measures
same as Back.
Bind off.

RIGHT FRONT
Lower Ribbing
Cast on and work in rib as for Left Front.

Body
Change to larger needle.
Continue to change color following
Stripe Sequence.
Row 1 (RS): K3{5, 7}, pm, work in K1, P1 Rib
as established over next 17 sts, pm, k5{7, 9}.
Row 2: Purl to marker, sm, work in K1, P1
Rib to next marker, sm, purl to end of row.
Row 3: Knit to marker, sm, work in K1, P1
Rib to next marker, sm, knit to end of row.
Row 4: Purl to marker, sm, work in K1, P1
Rib to next marker, sm, purl to end of row.
Rows 5-14: Rep Rows 2 and 3 for 5 times.
Row 15 (Decrease Row): Knit to marker,
sm, work in K1, P1 Rib to next marker, sm,
knit to last 3 sts, ssk, k1 – 24{28, 32} sts.
Rows 16-29: Rep Rows 2-15 – 23{27,
31} sts at the end of Row 29.
Rows 30 thru 31{33, 35}: Rep Rows 2
and 3 for 1{2, 3} times.

Join Pocket Lining
Remove markers while working next row.
Row 32{34, 36}: Purl to marker, bind off
17 sts between markers, purl to end of row.
Row 33{35, 37}: Knit to bound-off sts;
from RS, knit across sts of 2nd Pocket
Lining from st holder, knit to end of row.
Rows 34{36, 38} thru 42: Work in St st
for 9{7, 5} rows.
Row 43 (Decrease Row): Knit to last
3 sts, ssk, k1 – 22{26, 30} sts.
Rows 44 thru 48{54, 56}: Work in St st
for 5{11, 13} rows.

Size XS/S ONLY
Shape Neck
Row 49: K1, k2tog, knit to end of row –
21 sts.
Work in St st for 7 rows.

Row 57: Rep Row 43 – 20 sts.
Row 58: Purl.
Row 59: Rep Row 49 – 19 sts.
Work in St st for 9 rows.
Row 69: Rep Row 49 – 18 sts.
Row 70: Purl.
Row 71: Rep Row 43 – 17 sts.

Size M/L ONLY
Shape Neck
Row 55: K1, k2tog, knit to end of row –
25 sts.
Row 56: Purl.
Row 57: Rep Row 43 – 24 sts.
Work in St st for 7 rows.
Row 65: Rep Row 55 – 23 sts.
Work in St st for 5 rows.
Row 71: Rep Row 43 – 22 sts.

Size 1X/2X ONLY
Row 57: Rep Row 43 – 29 sts.
Work in St st for 3 rows.
Shape Neck
Row 61 (RS): K1, k2tog, knit to end of row –
28 sts.
Work in St st for 9 rows.
Row 71: K1, k2tog, knit to last 3 sts, ssk, k1 –
26 sts.

All Sizes
Work in St st for 7{3, 9} rows.
Row 79{75, 81}: K1, k2tog, knit to end of
row – 16{21, 25} sts.
Work in St st for 9 rows.
Row 89{85, 91}: K1, k2tog, knit to end of
row – 15{20, 24} sts.
Rep last 10 rows 0{1, 1} more time(s) –
15{19, 23} sts.
Work even in St st until piece measures
same as Back.
Bind off.

SLEEVES (MAKE 2)
Lower Ribbing
With smaller needle and A, cast on
25{27, 29} sts.
Work in rib as for Back.

Body
Change to larger needle.
Continuing to change color following
Stripe Sequence, work in St st for 3 rows.

Increase Row (RS): K1, M1, knit to last st, M1, k1 – 27{29, 31} sts.
Rep last 4 rows 11{12, 13} more times – 49{53, 57} sts.
Work even in St st until piece measures about 23" (58.5 cm) from beg.
Bind off.

FINISHING
Sew shoulder seams.

Front Bands and Collar
 Row 1 (RS): From RS with smaller needle and A, beg at lower right front corner, pick up and knit one st in end of each row along right front edge to beg of neck shaping, pm, pick up and knit one st in end of each row to right shoulder, pick up and knit one st in each st across back neck, pick up and knit one st in end of each row from left shoulder to beg of neck shaping, pm, pick up and knit one st in end of each row along left front edge to lower left front corner.

Work back and forth in rows on circular needle as if working with straight needles. Slip markers as you come to them.
Row 2: Work Row 1 of K1, P1 Rib.
Row 3: Work in K1, P1 Rib.
Row 4: Work in K1, P1 Rib to 10 sts before 2nd marker (marker on right front), TURN.
Row 5: Work in K1, P1 Rib to 10 sts before next marker (on left front), TURN.
Row 6: Work in K1, P1 Rib to end of row.
Row 7: Work in K1, P1 Rib.
Row 8: Work in K1, P1 Rib to 8 sts before 2nd marker (marker on right front), TURN.

Row 9: Work in K1, P1 Rib to 8 sts before next marker (on left front), TURN.
Row 10: Work in K1, P1 Rib to end of row.
Row 11: Work in K1, P1 Rib.
Row 12: Work in K1, P1 Rib to 6 sts before 2nd marker (marker on right front), TURN.
Row 13: Work in K1, P1 Rib to 6 sts before next marker (on left front), TURN.
Row 14: Work in K1, P1 Rib to end of row.
Row 15: Work in K1, P1 Rib.
Row 16: Work in K1, P1 Rib to 4 sts before 2nd marker (marker on right front), TURN.
Row 17: Work in K1, P1 Rib to 4 sts before next marker (on left front), TURN.
Row 18: Work in K1, p1 Rib to end of row.
Row 19: Work in K1, p1 Rib.
Row 20: Work in K1, p1 Rib to 2 sts before 2nd marker (marker on right front), TURN.
Row 21: Work in K1, p1 Rib to 2 sts before next marker (on left front), TURN.
Row 22: Work in K1, P1 Rib to end of row.
Row 23: Work in K1, P1 Rib.
Row 24: Work in K1, P1 Rib to 2nd marker (marker on right front), TURN.
Row 25: Work in K1, p1 Rib to next marker (on left front), TURN.
Row 26: Work in K1, P1 Rib to end of row.
Bind off in rib.

Sew in Sleeves. Sew Sleeve and side seams.
Sew Pocket Linings to WS of Fronts.
Weave in ends.

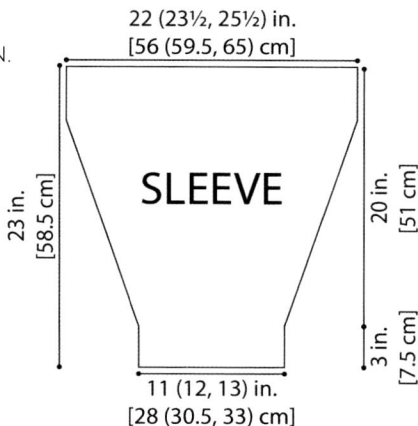

22 (23½, 25½) in.
[56 (59.5, 65) cm]

23 in.
[58.5 cm]

SLEEVE

20 in.
[51 cm]

3 in.
[7.5 cm]

11 (12, 13) in.
[28 (30.5, 33) cm]

FOLKE PULLOVER

■■□▷ **EASY**

SIZE

S{M/L, 1X/2}

Finished Bust: About 46{52, 58}"/ 117{132, 147.5} cm

Finished Length: About 18½{19½, 20½}"/47{49.5, 52} cm

Note: Pattern is written for smallest size with changes for larger sizes in braces. When only one number is given, it applies to all sizes.

To follow pattern more easily, circle all numbers pertaining to your size before beginning.

GAUGE

8 sts = about 4" (10 cm) in St st worked in the rnd (knit every st on every rnd).

BE SURE TO CHECK YOUR GAUGE.

SHOPPING LIST

SUPER BULKY 6

Yarn (Super Bulky Weight)
LION BRAND® WOOL-EASE® THICK & QUICK® (Art. #640)
- ☐ #124 Barley - 3{4, 5} balls (A)
- ☐ #143 Claret - 1{2, 2} ball(s) (B)
- ☐ #138 Cranberry - 1{2, 2} ball(s) (C)
- ☐ #153 Black - 1{2, 2} ball(s) (D)
- ☐ #099 Fisherman - 1{2, 2} ball(s) (E)

Knitting Needles
Circulars, 16" (40.5 cm), 24" (61 cm), 36" (91.5 cm) and 40" (101.5 cm) long,
- ☐ Size 13 (9 mm)
  or size needed for gauge

Additional Supplies
- ☐ LION BRAND® stitch markers
- ☐ LION BRAND® stitch holders
- ☐ LION BRAND® large-eyed blunt needle

NOTES

1. Pullover is worked in one piece, in the round, beginning at neck.

2. At underarms, piece is divided, then body and sleeves are worked separately. The body is worked in the round. The sleeves are worked back and forth in rows.

3. Stranded colorwork on the Pullover uses 2 colors on each round or row. Carry unused color loosely across WS of piece.

4. Colorwork can be worked by following written instructions or reading charts. Read all rows of body chart from right to left. Read RS rows of sleeve chart from right to left and WS rows from left to right.

5. Circular needles are used beg with the shortest circular needle. As sts are increased, longer circular needles are used.

6. When you see 'as established' in the instructions, this means to continue in the current pattern st. For example, to continue in a rib pattern, k the knit sts and p the purl sts.

7. When you see 'work even' in the instructions, this means to continue on in the pattern st you have established without changing the st count by increasing, decreasing, or binding off.

STITCH EXPLANATION
M1L (make 1 left leaning)
An increase worked by lifting the horizontal strand lying between needles and placing it onto the left needle. Knit this new stitch through the back loop – one st increased.

TECHNIQUE EXPLANATION
Cable Cast On
*Insert right needle between first 2 sts on left needle, wrap yarn and pull through (as if knitting a st), transfer new st to left needle; rep from * for desired number of sts.

PULLOVER
Yoke
With shortest circular needle and A, cast on 44{48, 52} sts.
Place marker for beg of rnd. Join by working the first st on the left hand needle with the working yarn from the right hand needle and being careful not to twist sts.
Knit 4 rnds.
Next Rnd: *K11{12, 13}, M1L; rep from * 3 more times – you will have 48{52, 56} sts in this rnd.

Begin Colorwork
Rnd 1: With A, k1, *with B, k1; with A, k3; rep from * to last 3 sts, with B, k1; with A, k2.
Rnd 2: *With B, k3; with A, k1; rep from * around.
Rnd 3: Rep Rnd 1.
Rnd 4 (Increase Rnd): *With C, k3; with A, k1, M1L; rep from * around – 60{65, 70} sts.
Rnds 5 and 6: *With C, k3; with A, k2; rep from * around.
Rnd 7 (Increase Rnd): With A, k4, *M1, k5; rep from * to last st, M1, k1 – 72 (78, 84) sts.
Rnd 8: With A, k1, *with D, k1; with A, k5; rep from * to last 5 sts, with D, k1; with A, k4.
Rnd 9: *With D, k3; with A, k3; rep from * around.
Rnd 10: With D, k4, *with A, k1; with D, k5; rep from * to last 2 sts, with A, k1; with D, k1.
Rnd 11 (Increase Rnd): With D, k5, *M1L, k6; rep from * to last st, M1L, k1 – 84{91, 98} sts.
Rnd 12: With D, k1, *with B, k1; with D, k6; rep from * to last 6 sts, with B, k1; with D, k5.
Rnd 13: *With B, k3; with D, k4; rep from * around.

Rnd 14: With B, k4, *with D, k2; with B, k5; rep from * to last 3 sts, with D, k2; with B, k1.
Rnd 15 (Increase Rnd): With B, k1, *with A, k1; with B, k3; with A, M1L; with B, k3; rep from * to last 6 sts, with A, k1; with B, k3; with A, M1L; with B, k2 – 96{104, 112} sts.
Rnd 16: *With A, k3; with B, k1; rep from * around.
Rnd 17: *With E, k1; with A, k1; rep from * around.
Rnd 18: *With A, k1; with E, k1; rep from * around.
Rnd 19 (Increase Rnd): *With C, k8{6, 5}, M1L; rep from * 11{15, 19} more times, knit to end of rnd – 108{120, 132} sts.
Rnds 20 and 21: *With B, k2; with C, k2; rep from * around.
Rnds 22 and 23: With A, k1; *with D, k4; with A, k2; rep from * to last 5 sts, with D, k4; with A, k1.
Rnds 24 and 25: With A, k2, *with D, k2; with A, k4; rep from * to last 4 sts, with D, k2; with A, k2.
Rnds 26 and 27: With A, k1, *with E, k4; with A, k2; rep from * to last 5 sts, with E, k4; with A, k1.
Rnd 28 (Increase Rnd): *With A, k9{10, 11}, M1L; rep from * around – 120{132, 144} sts.
Rnd 29: With A, k1, *with C, k1; with A, k3; rep from * to last 3 sts, with C, k1; with A, k2.
Rnd 30: *With C, k3; with A, k1; rep from * around.
Rnd 31: Rep Rnd 29.
Rnds 32-34: *With B, k3; with A, k1; rep from * around.

For Size S ONLY
Cut B and C.
Proceed to Divide for Body and Sleeves.

For Size M/L ONLY
Rnds 35-37: Rep Rnds 29-31.
Cut B and C.
Proceed to Divide for Body and Sleeves.

For Size 1X/2X ONLY
Rnds 35-40: Rep Rnds 29-34.
Cut B and C.
Proceed to Divide for Body and Sleeves.

Divide for Body and Sleeves
Dividing Rnd: Place first 20{22, 24} sts onto a st holder for first sleeve; with A,

Online shopping just got easier!

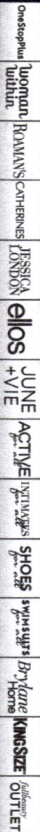

OUR FAMILY OF BRANDS, ALL IN ONE PLACE

1 Order • 1 Fast Checkout

bonus savings

30% OFF

ANY ORDER OF $150+ WHEN YOU SHOP 2 OR MORE BRANDS

USE CODE: **OSPFAMILY**

*See back for details

OneStopPlus
Woman Within
ROAMAN'S
CATHERINES
JESSICA LONDON
ellos
JUNE + VIE
ACTIVE for all
INTIMATES for all
SHOES for all
SWIMSUITS for all
BrylaneHome
KingSize
fullbeauty OUTLET

TRY IT TODAY Go to your favorite brand's website to get your discount!*

Online shopping just got easier!

our family of brands

1 order • 1 fast checkout

ROMAN'S
romans.com

ellos
ellos.us

JUNE
+VIE
juneandvie.com

KINGSIZE
kingsize.com

SWIMSUITS
for all
swimsuitsforall.com

SHOES
for all
shoesforall.com

fullbeauty
OUTLET
fullbeauty.com

woman within
womanwithin.com

JESSICA LONDON
jessicalondon.com

CATHERINES
catherines.com

BryLaneHome
brylanehome.com

INTIMATES
for all
intimatesforall.com

ACTIVE
for all
activeforall.com

OneStopPlus
onestopplus.com

30% OFF

ANY ORDER OF $150+
WHEN YOU SHOP
2 OR MORE BRANDS

USE CODE:

OSPFAMILY

*Details below

- Register your mattress: beautyrest.com/register

- Receive an entry into our monthly sweepstakes by registering your product online.

- If you have questions about your warranty, please use our website to access the full terms: beautyrest.com/warranties

- **To receive service under the terms of the warranty, contact your original Beautyrest® dealer. If the dealer is no longer in business or you have moved outside its service area, see below to contact Simmons Consumer Services.**

- To receive a paper copy of your warranty, see below to contact Simmons Consumer Services.

Phone: 1-877-399-9397
Email: customerassistance@simmons.com
Address: Simmons Consumer Services
One Concourse Parkway, Suite 800
Atlanta, GA 30328

Beautyrest

Beautyrest®

CONGRATULATIONS ON YOUR
NEW BEAUTYREST® MATTRESS!

Register your mattress now
for a chance TO WIN!

See back for details.

cable cast on 6{8, 10} sts for underarm, k40{44, 48}, place next 20{22, 24} sts onto a st holder for second sleeve, cable cast on 6{8, 10} sts for underarm, k40{44, 48} – 92{104, 116} sts on needle for body. Place marker for beg of rnd and join to work in the rnd.

Body
Rnd 1: *With A, k1; with D, k1; rep from * around.
Rnd 2: *With D, k1; with A, k1; rep from * around.
Rnd 3: With A, knit.
Rnd 4: With A, k1, *with E, k1; with A, k3; rep from * to last 3 sts, with E, k1; with A, k2.
Rnd 5: *With E, k3; with A, k1; rep from * around.
Rnd 6: Rep Rnd 4.
Cut D and E. Continue with A only.
Rnd 7: Knit.

Ribbing
Rnds 8-15: *K1, p1; rep from * around.
Bind off in rib.

SLEEVES
Slip 20{22, 24} sleeve sts from one st holder onto shortest circular needle.
Row 1 (RS): From RS with A, cable cast on 4{5, 6} sts, knit the sts just cast on, k20{22, 24} sleeve sts – 24{27, 30} sts.
Row 2: With A, cable cast on 4{5, 6} sts, purl the sts just cast on, purl to end of row – 28{32, 36} sts.

Row 3: *With A, k1; with D, k1; rep from * across.
Row 4: *With D, p1; with A, p1; rep from * across.
Row 5: With A, knit.
Row 6: With A, p1, *with E, p1; with A, p3; rep from * to last 3 sts, with E, p1; with A, p2.
Row 7: *With E, k3; with A, k1; rep from * across.
Row 8: *With D, p1; with A, p1; rep from * across.
Cut B, D, and E. Continue with A only.
Row 9: With A, knit.

Ribbing
Row 10 (WS): *K1, p1; rep from * across.
Row 11 (Decrease Row): P1, k2tog, knit the knit sts and purl the purl sts to last 3 sts, p2tog, k1 – 26{30, 34} sts.
Rows 12-16: Knit the knit sts and purl the purl sts.
Row 17 (Decrease Row): K1, p2tog, knit the knit sts and purl the purl sts to last 3 sts, k2tog, p1 – 24{28, 32} sts.
Rows 18-22: Rep Rows 12-16.
Row 23: Rep Row 11 – 22{26, 30} sts.
Row 24: Knit the knit sts and purl the purl sts.
Rep Row 24 until sleeve measures about 14{15, 16}"/35.5{38, 40.5} cm from underarm.
Bind off all sts in rib.
Rep for second sleeve.

FINISHING
Sew sleeve and underarm seams.
Weave in ends.

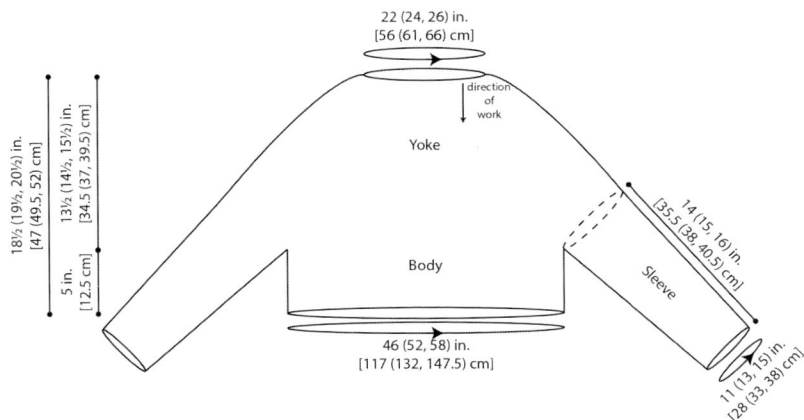

22 (24, 26) in.
[56 (61, 66) cm]

direction of work

Yoke

18½ (19½, 20½) in.
[47 (49.5, 52) cm]

13½ (14½, 15½) in.
[34.5 (37, 39.5) cm]

5 in.
[12.5 cm]

Body

14 (15, 16) in.
[35.5 (38, 40.5) cm]

Sleeve

46 (52, 58) in.
[117 (132, 147.5) cm]

11 (13, 15) in.
[28 (33, 38) cm]

DAGNY PULLOVER

■■□▭ **EASY**

SIZE

S/M{L, 1X/2X}
Finished Bust: About 48{54, 60}"/
122{137, 152.5} cm
Finished Length: About 28½{29½,
30½}"/72.5{75, 77.5} cm)

Note: Pattern is written for smallest size
with changes for larger sizes in braces.
When only one number is given, it
applies to all sizes.
To follow pattern more easily, circle all
numbers pertaining to your size before
beginning.

GAUGE

9 sts = about 4¼ (11 cm);
14 rows = about 4½" (11.5 cm) in St st
(knit on RS, purl on WS) with A.

BE SURE TO CHECK YOUR GAUGE.

SHOPPING LIST 🔲SUPER BULKY 6

Yarn (Super Bulky Weight)
LION BRAND® HOMESPUN®
THICK & QUICK® (Art. #792)
☐ #412 Pearls - 1{2, 2} skein(s) (A)
LION BRAND® WOOL-EASE®
THICK & QUICK® (Art. #640)
☐ #099 Fisherman - 5{6, 7} balls (B)

Knitting Needles
Circulars, 16" (40.5 cm)
and 40" (101.5 cm) long,
☐ Size 11 (8 mm)
or size needed for gauge

Additional Supplies
☐ LION BRAND® stitch markers
☐ LION BRAND® stitch holders
☐ LION BRAND® large-eyed
blunt needle

NOTES

1. Pullover is worked in 4 pieces: Back, Front, and 2 Sleeves.

2. Each piece is worked with purl ridges in Color Ridges pattern.

3. The longer circular needle is used to accommodate the sts. Work back and forth in rows on the circular needle as if working on straight needles.

4. The shorter circular needle is used for the ribbed neck.

5. When you see 'work in pattern as established' in the instructions, this means to work the next row of the current pattern.

6. When you see 'work even' in the instructions, this means to continue on in the pattern st you have established without changing the st count by increasing, decreasing, or binding off.

7. For smallest size only, divide yarn A into 2 separate balls before beginning.

STITCH EXPLANATIONS
M1L (make 1 left leaning)
An increase worked by lifting the horizontal strand lying between needles and placing it onto the left needle. Knit this new stitch through the back loop – one st increased.

M1P (make 1 as if to purl)
An increase worked by lifting the horizontal strand lying between needles and placing it onto the left needle. Purl this new stitch through the back loop – one st increased.

CDD (centered double decrease)
Slip 2 as if to knit 2 together, knit 1, pass 2 slipped stitches over – 2 sts decreased.

ssk (slip, slip, knit)
Slip next 2 sts as if to knit, one at a time, to right hand needle; insert left hand needle into fronts of these 2 sts and knit them together – one st decreased.

PATTERN STITCHES
K1, P1 Rib
(worked over an odd number of sts)
Row 1: K1, *p1, k1; rep from * to end of row.
Row 2: Knit the knit sts and purl the purl sts. Rep Row 2 for K1, P1 Rib.

COLOR RIDGES PATTERN
Rows 1-10: With B, beg with a RS (knit) row, work in St st (knit on RS, purl on WS) for 10 rows.
Row 11 (RS): With A, purl.
Row 12: With A, knit.
Rep Rows 1-12 for Color Ridges pattern.

BACK
With longer circular needle and A, cast on 51{57, 63} sts.
Work in K1, P1 Rib for 3 rows.

Beg with a RS (knit) row, work in St st (knit on RS, purl on WS) until piece measures about 5" (12.5 cm) from beg, end with a WS row as the last row you work.

First Purl Ridge
Next Row (RS): Purl.
Next Row: Knit.

Join B.
Beginning with Row 1 of pattern, work in Color Ridges pattern until piece measures about 27{28, 29}"/68.5{71, 73.5} cm from beg, end with a WS row as the last row you work.
Cut A and continue with B only.

Shape Neck and Shoulders
Row 1 (RS): K19{21, 23} sts for right shoulder, join a second ball of yarn and bind off center 13{15, 17} sts, knit to end of row for left shoulder – 19{21, 23} sts for each shoulder.

You will now work both shoulders AT THE SAME TIME with separate balls of yarn.
Row 2: On left shoulder, bind off 9{10, 11} sts, purl to end; on right shoulder, bind off 2 sts, purl to end.
Row 3: On right shoulder, bind off 9{10, 11} sts, knit to end; on left shoulder, bind off 2 sts, knit to end – 8{9, 10} sts for each shoulder.
Row 4: On left shoulder, bind off rem 8{9, 10} sts; on right shoulder, purl to end.
Bind off rem 8{9, 10} sts of right shoulder.

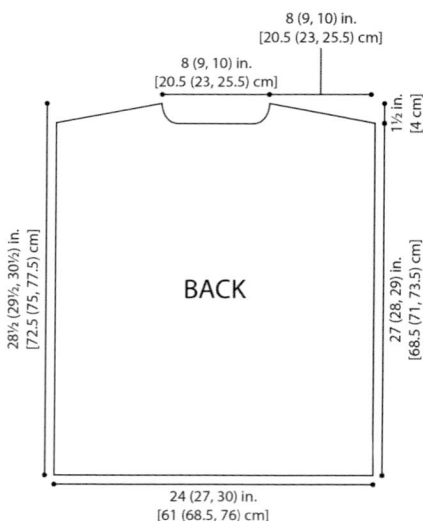

8 (9, 10) in.
[20.5 (23, 25.5) cm]

8 (9, 10) in.
[20.5 (23, 25.5) cm]

1½ in.
[4 cm]

28½ (29½, 30½) in.
[72.5 (75, 77.5) cm]

BACK

27 (28, 29) in.
[68.5 (71, 73.5) cm]

24 (27, 30) in.
[61 (68.5, 76) cm]

FRONT

Work same as Back until piece measures about 18{19, 20}"/45.5{48.5, 51} cm from beg, end with a WS row as the last row you work.

Shape Neck

Row 1 (RS): Work in Color Ridges pattern as established over first 25{28, 31} sts for left shoulder, join a second ball of yarn and bind off center st, work in Color Ridges pattern as established to end of row for right shoulder – 25{28, 31} sts for each shoulder.

You will now work both shoulders AT THE SAME TIME with separate balls of yarn.
Row 2: Work in Color Ridges pattern across both shoulders, using separate balls of yarn.
Row 3: On left shoulder, work in Color Ridges pattern to last 3 sts, k2tog, k1; on right shoulder, k1, ssk, work in Color Ridges pattern to end – 24{27, 30} sts for each shoulder.
Rows 4-6: Work even in Color Ridges pattern over both shoulders, using separate balls of yarn, for 3 rows.
Row 7: Rep Row 3 – 23{26, 29} sts for each shoulder.
Rows 8-13: Rep Rows 2-7 – 21{24, 27} sts for each shoulder.

Work even in Color Ridges pattern as established over both shoulders, using separate balls of yarn, until piece measures about 25{25½, 26}"/63.5{65, 66} cm, end with a WS row as the last row you work.

Next Row (RS): On left shoulder, work in Color Ridges pattern to last 3 sts, k2tog, k1; on right shoulder, k1, ssk, work in Color Ridges pattern to end – 20{23, 26} sts for each shoulder.
Next Row: Work even in Color Ridges pattern over both shoulders, using separate balls of yarn.
Rep last 2 rows 2{3, 4} more times – 18{20, 22} sts.
Cut A.

Shape Shoulders and Continue Shaping Neck

Work with B only to end of piece.
Row 1 (RS): On left shoulder, bind off 9{10, 11} sts, knit to last 3 sts, k2tog, k1; on right shoulder, k1, ssk, knit to end.
Row 2: On right shoulder, bind off 9{10, 11} sts, purl to end; on left shoulder, purl to end – 8{9, 10} sts for each shoulder.
Row 3: On left shoulder, bind off rem 8{9, 10} sts; on right shoulder, knit to end.
Bind off rem 8{9, 10} sts of right shoulder.

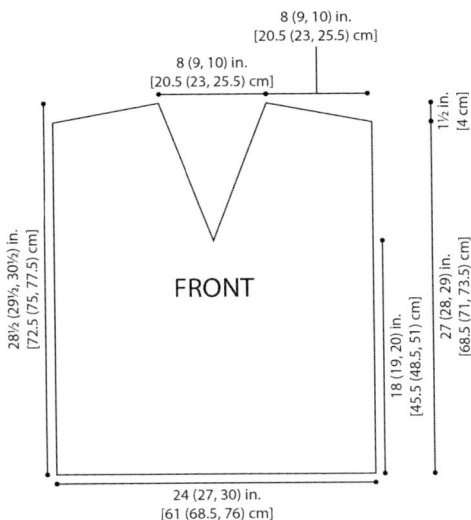

8 (9, 10) in.
[20.5 (23, 25.5) cm]

8 (9, 10) in.
[20.5 (23, 25.5) cm]

1½ in.
[4 cm]

28½ (29½, 30½) in.
[72.5 (75, 77.5) cm]

FRONT

27 (28, 29) in.
[68.5 (71, 73.5) cm]

18 (19, 20) in.
[45.5 (48.5, 51) cm]

24 (27, 30) in.
[61 (68.5, 76) cm]

SLEEVES (MAKE 2)

With longer circular needle and A, cast on 27{29, 31} sts.
Work in K1, P1 Rib for 3 rows.

Beg with a RS (knit) row, work in St st until piece measures about 5" (12.5 cm) from beg, end with a WS (purl) row as the last row you work.

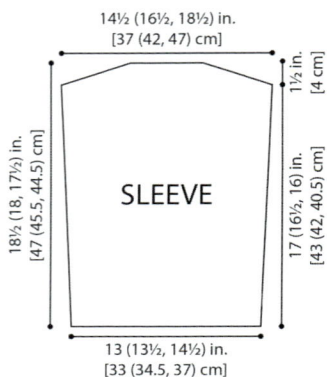

14½ (16½, 18½) in.
[37 (42, 47) cm]

1½ in.
[4 cm]

18½ (18, 17½) in.
[47 (45.5, 44.5) cm]

SLEEVE

17 (16½, 16) in.
[43 (42, 40.5) cm]

13 (13½, 14½) in.
[33 (34.5, 37) cm]

First Purl Ridge
Next Row (RS): Purl.
Next Row: Knit.
Change to B.

Size S/M ONLY
Rows 1-9: Work Rows 1-9 of Color Ridges pattern.
Row 10 (Increase Row): With B, p1, M1P, purl to last st, M1P, P1 – 29 sts.
Row 11: With A, purl.
Row 12: With A, knit.
Rep Rows 1-12 – 31 sts.
Work even in Color Ridges pattern as established until piece measures about 17" (43 cm) from beg, end with a WS row as the last row you work.
Proceed to Shape Cap (Top of Sleeve).

Size L ONLY
Rows 1-3: Work Rows 1-3 of Color Ridges pattern.
Row 4 (Increase Row): With B, p1, M1P, purl to last st, M1P, P1 – 31 sts.
Rows 5-9: Work Rows 5-9 of Color Ridges pattern.
Row 10: Rep Row 4 – 33 sts.
Row 11: With A, purl.
Row 12: With A, knit.
Rep Rows 1-4 – 35 sts.
Work even in Color Ridges pattern as established until piece measures about 16½" (42 cm) from beg, end with a WS row as the last row you work.
Proceed to Shape Cap (Top of Sleeve).

Size 1X/2X ONLY
Row 1: Work Row 1 of Color Ridges pattern.
Row 2 (Increase Row): With B, p1, M1P, p to last st, M1P, P1 – 33 sts.
Rows 3-5: Work Rows 3-5 of Color Ridges pattern.
Row 6: Rep Row 2 – 35 sts.
Rows 7-9: Work Rows 7-9 of Color Ridges pattern.
Row 10: Rep Row 2 – 37 sts.
Row 11: With A, purl.

Row 12: With A, knit.
Rep Rows 1 and 2 – 39 sts.
Work even in Color Ridges pattern as established until piece measures about 16" (40.5 cm) from beg, end with a WS row as the last row you work.
Proceed to Shape Cap (Top of Sleeve).

Shape Cap (Top of Sleeve)
Work with B only to end of piece.

Row 1 (RS): Bind off 5{6, 7} sts, knit to end of row – 26{29, 32} sts.
Row 2: Bind off 5{6, 7} sts, purl to end of row – 21{23, 25} sts.
Rows 3 and 4: Rep Rows 1 and 2 – 11 sts.
Bind off rem 11 sts.

FINISHING
Sew shoulder seams.

Ribbed Neck
From RS, with shorter needle and B, beg at left shoulder seam, pick up and knit 18 sts evenly spaced along left front neck edge, one st at center front neck, 18 sts along right front neck edge, and 19{21, 23} sts across back neck – 56{58, 60} sts.
Place marker and join by working the first st on the left needle with the working yarn from the right needle.
Rnd 1: K1, *p1, k1; rep from * to 1 st before center front st, CDD, place marker (pm) on st just made, **k1, p1; rep from ** to end of rnd.
Rnds 2-6: Knit the knit sts and purl the purl sts to one st before marked st, CDD, pm on st just made, knit the knits sts and purl the purl sts to end of rnd.
Bind off in rib.

Place markers on side edges of Back and Front, about 7{8, 9}"/18{20.5, 23} cm below shoulder seams.
Sew tops of Sleeves between markers.
Sew side and Sleeve seams.

Weave in ends.

PETRINE CARDIGAN

◼◼◼◻ INTERMEDIATE

SIZE

S/M{L, 1X/2X}

Finished Bust: About 34½{39, 42½, 47, 51½}"/87.5{99, 108, 119.5, 131} cm, unbuttoned

Finished Length: About 25½{26, 26½, 27, 27½}"/65{66, 67.5, 68.5, 70} cm, including neckband

Note: Pattern is written for smallest size with changes for larger sizes in braces. When only one number is given, it applies to all sizes. To follow pattern more easily, circle all numbers pertaining to your size before beginning.

GAUGE

16 sts = about 3" (7.5 cm); 25 rows = about 4" (10 cm) in Twin Rib pattern.

BE SURE TO CHECK YOUR GAUGE.

SHOPPING LIST

Yarn (Medium Weight) 🧶4

LION BRAND® JEANS® (Art. #505)

☐ #109 Stonewash - 5{5, 6, 7, 7} balls (A)

☐ #105 Faded - 1{1, 1, 2, 2} ball(s) (B)

☐ #121 Top Stitch - 1{1, 1, 2, 2} ball(s) (C)

☐ #110 Classic - 1{1, 1, 1, 1} ball (D)

☐ #153 Stovepipe - 1{1, 1, 2, 2} ball(s) (E)

Knitting Needles

Circular, 40" (101.5 cm) long,

☐ Size 8 (5 mm)

or size needed for gauge

Additional Supplies

☐ LION BRAND® stitch markers

☐ LION BRAND® stitch holders

☐ LION BRAND® large-eyed blunt needle

☐ 1" (2.5 cm) diameter Buttons - 5

NOTES

1. Cardigan is worked in 3 pieces: Body and 2 Sleeves.

2. Lower edge of Sleeves and Body are worked in a Twin Rib pattern.

3. The Sleeves are worked first, then the Body is worked from lower edge up to underarms. At underarms, the piece is divided for fronts and back and Sleeves are joined.

4. The Yoke is worked in 3 different colorwork patterns. Colorwork can be worked by following the written instructions or the charts. When working from charts, read RS rows from right to left and WS rows from left to right.

5. Ribbed front bands are worked in one with the Body and yoke.

6. A circular needle is used to accommodate the number of sts in the Body. Work back and forth in rows on the circular needle just as if working on straight needles.

7. When you see 'work in pattern as established' in the instructions, this means to work the next row of the pattern sts, lining up sts as in previous rows.

8. When you see 'work even' in the instructions, this means to continue on in the pattern st you have established without changing the st count by increasing, decreasing, or binding off.

STITCH EXPLANATION

M1L (make 1)
An increase worked by lifting the horizontal strand lying between needles and placing it onto the left needle. Knit this new stitch through the back loop – one st increased.

PATTERN STITCHES

Twin Rib (worked over a multiple of 6 sts)
Row 1 (RS): *K3, p3; rep from * to end.
Row 2: *P1, k1; rep from * to end.
Rep Rows 1 and 2 for Twin Rib pattern.

K1, P1 Rib
(worked over an odd number of sts)
Row 1: K1, *p1, k1; rep from * to end of row.
Row 2: Knit the knit sts and purl the purl sts.
Rep Row 2 for K1, P1 Rib.

SLEEVES (MAKE 2)
With A, cast on 54{54, 54, 60, 60} sts. Beg with a WS (purl) row, work in St st (knit on RS, purl on WS) for 7 rows. Beg with Row 1 of pattern, work in Twin Rib for 10{8, 4, 4, 2} rows.

Increase Row (RS): Work one st in Twin Rib pattern as established, M1L, work in Twin Rib pattern as established to last st, M1L, work last st in Twin Rib pattern as established – you will have 56{56, 56, 62, 62} sts in this row.
Work even in Twin Rib pattern as established, working new sts into pattern, for 9{7, 3, 3, 1} row(s).
Rep last 10{8, 4, 4, 2} rows for 0{2, 5, 6, 11} more times – 56{60, 66, 74, 84} sts.
Work even in Twin Rib pattern as established until piece measures about 16{16, 16½, 16½, 16½}"/40.5{40.5, 42, 42, 42} cm from beg, end with a WS row as the last row you work.

Next 2 Rows: Bind off 5{6, 6, 8, 9} sts, work in Twin Rib pattern as established to end of row – 46{48, 54, 58, 66} sts when all bind offs have been completed.
Place rem 46{48, 54, 58, 66} sts on a st holder.

BODY
With A, cast on 185{209, 227, 251, 275} sts.

Row 1 (RS): Work Row 1 of K1, P1 Rib over first 7 sts for right front band, place marker (pm), work Row 1 of Twin Rib pattern to last 10 sts, k3, pm, work Row 1 of K1, P1 Rib over last 7 sts for left front band.
Row 2: Work in K1, P1 Rib as established to first marker, slip marker (sm), k1, work Row 2 of Twin Rib pattern to next marker, sm, work in K1, P1 Rib as established to end of row.
Row 3: Work in K1, P1 Rib as established to first marker, slip marker (sm), work Row 1 of Twin Rib pattern to 3 sts before marker, k3, sm, work in K1, P1 Rib as established to end of row.
Rep Rows 2 and 3 until piece measures about 14" (35.5 cm) from beg, end with a WS row as the last row you work.

Divide for Fronts and Back
Next Row (RS): Work in K1, P1 Rib as established to first marker, sm, work in Twin Rib pattern as established over next 36{42, 46, 51, 56} sts for right front, bind off 10{12, 12, 16, 18} sts for underarm, continue in Twin Rib pattern as established over next 78{86, 96, 102, 112} sts (you'll have 79{87, 97, 103, 113} sts for back), bind off next 10{12, 12, 16, 18} sts for underarm, work in Twin Rib pattern as established to next marker for left front, sm, work in K1, P1 Rib as established to end of row – 165{185, 203, 219, 239} sts.

Yoke
Next Row (Joining Row – WS): Work in K1, P1 Rib as established to first marker, sm, purl the left front sts, purl 46{48, 54, 58, 66} sts of one sleeve from st holder, purl the back sts, purl 46{48, 54, 58, 66} sts of 2nd sleeve from st holder, purl the right front sts, sm, work in K1, P1 Rib as established to end of row – 257{281, 311, 335, 371} sts.
Keeping sts of front bands in K1, P1 Rib as established, work even in St st for 0{2, 4, 8, 12} rows.

Next Row (Buttonhole Row – RS): K1, p1, k1, yo, k2tog (for buttonhole), p1, k1, sm, knit to last marker, sm, work in K1, P1 Rib as established to end of row.
Next Row: Work in K1, P1 Rib as established to first marker, sm, purl to last marker, p1, (k1, p1) 3 times.

CHARTED PATTERNS
Chart 1
Row 1 (RS): With A, work in K1, P1 Rib to first marker, sm; with E, k2, *with E, k2; with B, k1; with E, k3; rep from * to one st before last marker; with E, k1, sm; with A, work in K1, P1 Rib to end of row.
Row 2: With A, work in K1, P1 Rib to first marker, sm; with E, p1, *with E, p2; with B, p3; with E, p1; rep from * to 2 sts before last marker; with E, p2, sm; with A, work in K1, P1 Rib to end of row.
Row 3: With A, work in K1, P1 Rib to first marker, sm; with E, k2, *(with B, k2; with E, k1) twice; rep from * to one st before last marker; with E, k1, sm; with A, work in K1, P1 Rib to end of row.
Row 4: Rep Row 2.
Row 5: Rep Row 1.
Row 6: With A, work in K1, P1 Rib to first marker, sm; with E, purl to last marker, sm; with A, work in K1, P1 Rib to end of row.
Row 7: With A, work in K1, P1 Rib to first marker, sm; with C, k2, *with E, k5; with C, k1; rep from * to one st before last marker; with C, k1, sm; with A, work in K1, P1 Rib to end of row.
Row 8: With A, work in K1, P1 Rib to first marker, sm; with C, p1, *with C, p2; with E, p3; with C, p1; rep from * to 2 sts before last marker; with C, p2, sm; with A, work in K1, P1 Rib to end of row.
Row 9: With A, work in K1, P1 Rib to first marker, sm; with C, k2, *(with E, k1; with C, k1) 3 times; rep from * to one st before last marker; with C, k1, sm; with A, work in K1, P1 Rib to end of row.
Row 10: With A, work in K1, P1 Rib to first marker, sm; with C, p1, *with C, p2; (with E, p1; with C, p1) twice; rep from * to 2 sts before last marker; with C, p2, sm; with A, work in K1, P1 Rib to end of row.

Chart 1

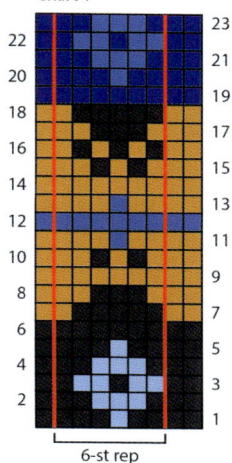

6-st rep

COLOR KEY
- #109 Stonewash (A)
- #105 Faded (B)
- #121 Top Stitch (C)
- #110 Classic (D)
- #153 Stovepipe (E)

Row 11: With A, work in K1, P1 Rib to first marker, sm; with C, k2, *with C, k2; with A, k1; with C, k3; rep from * to one st before last marker; with C, k1, sm; with A, work in K1, P1 Rib to end of row.
Row 12: With A, work in K1, P1 Rib to first marker, sm; with A, purl to last marker, sm; with A, work in K1, P1 Rib to end of row.
Row 13: Rep Row 11.
Row 14: With A, work in K1, P1 Rib to first marker, sm; with C, purl to last marker, sm; with A, work in K1, P1 Rib to end of row.
Row 15 (Buttonhole Row): With A, k1, p1, k1, yo, k2tog, p1, k1, sm; with C, k2, *(with C, k1; with E, k1) twice; with C, k2; rep from * to one st before last marker; with C, k1, sm; with A, work in K1, P1 Rib to end of row.
Row 16: With A, work in K1, P1 Rib to first marker, sm; with C, p1, *(with C, p1; with E, p1) 3 times; rep from * to 2 sts before last marker; with C, p2, sm; with A, p1, (k1, p1) 3 times.

last marker; with D, k1, sm; with A, work in K1, P1 Rib to end of row.

Row 22: With A, work in K1, P1 Rib to first marker, sm; with D, p1, *(with D, p1; with A, p2) twice; rep from * to 2 sts before last marker; with D, p2, sm; with A, work in K1, P1 Rib to end of row.

Row 23: Rep Row 21.

Next Row (Decrease Row): With A, work in K1, P1 Rib to first marker, sm; with D, p1, *with D, p2tog, p1; with A, p1; with D, p2; rep from * 37{43, 43, 49, 55} more times, (with D, p3; with A, p1; with D, p2) 2{0, 5, 3, 3} times to 2 sts before last marker; with D, p2tog, sm; with A, work in K1, P1 Rib to end of row – 218{236, 266, 284, 314} sts.

Chart 2

Row 1 (RS): With A, work in K1, P1 Rib to first marker, sm; with D, knit to last marker, sm; with A, work in K1, P1 Rib to end of row.

Row 2: With A, work in K1, P1 Rib to first marker, sm; *with B, p1; with E, p3; with B, p1; with E, p1; rep from * to last marker, sm; with A, work in K1, P1 Rib to end of row.

Row 3: With A, work in K1, P1 Rib to first marker, sm; *with B, k3; with E, k1; with B, k2; rep from * to last marker, sm; with A, work in K1, P1 Rib to end of row.

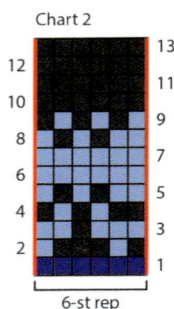

Row 17: With A, work in K1, P1 Rib to first marker, sm; with C, k2, *with C, k1; with E, k3; with C, k2; rep from * to one st before last marker; with C, k1, sm; with A, work in K1, P1 Rib to end of row.

Row 18: With A, work in K1, P1 Rib to first marker, sm; with C, p1, *with C, p1; with E, p5; rep from * to 2 sts before last marker; with C, p2, sm; with A, work in K1, P1 Rib to end of row.

Row 19: With A, work in K1, P1 Rib to first marker, sm; with D, knit to last marker, sm; with A, work in K1, P1 Rib to end of row.

Row 20: With A, work in K1, P1 Rib to first marker, sm; with D, p1, *with D, p3; with A, p1; with D, p2; rep from * to 2 sts before last marker; with D, p2, sm; with A, work in K1, P1 Rib to end of row.

Row 21: With A, work in K1, P1 Rib to first marker, sm; with D, k2, *with D, k1; with A, k3; with D, k2; rep from * to one st before

Chart 2

6-st rep

COLOR KEY

■	#109 Stonewash (A)
☐	#105 Faded (B)
■	#121 Top Stitch (C)
■	#110 Classic (D)
■	#153 Stovepipe (E)

Row 4: With A, work in K1, P1 Rib to first marker, sm; *(with E, p1; with B, p1) twice; with E, p2; rep from * to last marker, sm; with A, work in K1, P1 Rib to end of row.

Row 5: With A, work in K1, P1 Rib to first marker, sm; *with B, k2; (with E, k1; with B, k1) twice; rep from * to last marker, sm; with A, work in K1, P1 Rib to end of row.

Row 6: With A, work in K1, P1 Rib to first marker, sm; with B, purl to last marker, sm; with A, work in K1, P1 Rib to end of row.

Row 7: With A, work in K1, P1 Rib to first marker, sm; with B, knit to last marker, sm; with A, work in K1, P1 Rib to end of row.

Row 8: With A, work in K1, P1 Rib to first marker, sm; *(with B, p1; with E, p1) twice; with B, p2; rep from * to last marker, sm; with A, work in K1, P1 Rib to end of row.

Row 9 (Buttonhole Row): With A, k1, p1, k1, yo, k2tog, p1, k1, sm; *(with B, k1; with E, k1) 3 times; rep from * to last marker, sm; with A, work in K1, P1 Rib to end of row.

Row 10: With A, work in K1, P1 Rib to first marker, sm; with E, purl to last marker, sm; with A, work in K1, P1 Rib to end of row.

Row 11: With A, work in K1, P1 Rib to first marker, sm; with E, knit to last marker, sm; with A, work in K1, P1 Rib to end of row.

Rows 12 and 13: Rep Rows 10 and 11.

Next Row (Decrease Row): With A, work in K1, P1 Rib to first marker, sm; with E, p4{3, 11, 11, 8}, p2tog, (p1, p2tog, p2{2, 1, 1, 1}, p2tog, p1, p2tog) 19{21, 25, 27, 31} times, p1, p2tog, p to last marker, sm; with A, work in K1, P1 Rib to end of row – 159{171, 189, 201, 219} sts.

Chart 3

Row 1 (RS): With A, work in K1, P1 Rib to first marker, sm; with E, k1, *with E, k2; with C, k1; with E, k3; rep from * to last marker, sm; with A, work in K1, P1 Rib to end of row.

Row 2: With A, work in K1, P1 Rib to first marker, sm; *with E, p2; with C, p3; with E, p1; rep from * to one st before last marker; with E, p1, sm; with A, work in K1, P1 Rib to end of row.

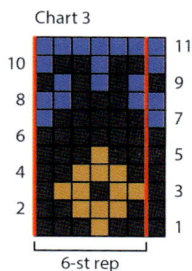

Chart 3

6-st rep

COLOR KEY
- #109 Stonewash (A)
- #105 Faded (B)
- #121 Top Stitch (C)
- #110 Classic (D)
- #153 Stovepipe (E)

Row 3: With A, work in K1, P1 Rib to first marker, sm; with E, k1, *(with C, k2; with E, k1) twice; rep from * to last marker, sm; with A, work in K1, P1 Rib to end of row.

Row 4: Rep Row 2.

Row 5: Rep Row 1.

Row 6: With A, work in K1, P1 Rib to first marker, sm; with E, purl to last marker, sm; with A, work in K1, P1 Rib to end of row.

Row 7: With A, work in K1, P1 Rib to first marker, sm; with A, k1, *with E, k5; with A, k1; rep from * to last marker, sm; with A, work in K1, P1 Rib to end of row.

Row 8: With A, work in K1, P1 Rib to first marker, sm; *with A, p2; with E, p3; with A, p1; rep from * to one st before last marker; with A, p1, sm; with A, work in K1, P1 Rib to end of row.

Row 9 (Buttonhole Row): With A, k1, p1, k1, yo, k2tog, p1, k1, sm; with E, k1, *(with A, k1; with E, k1) 3 times; rep from * to last marker, sm; with A, work in K1, P1 Rib to end of row.

Row 10: With A, work in K1, P1 Rib to first marker, sm; *(with A, p1; with E, p2) twice; rep from * to one st before last marker; with A, p1, sm; with A, p1, (k1, p1) 3 times.

Row 11: With A, work in K1, P1 Rib to first marker, sm; with A, knit to last marker, sm; with A, work in K1, P1 Rib to end of row.

Next Row (Decrease Row): With A, work in K1, P1 Rib to first marker, sm; with A, *p2{1, 1, 1, 1}, (p2tog) 3 times; rep from * 16{19, 23, 24, 27} more times, p3{6, 3, 5, 2}, (p2tog) 1{2, 0, 1, 2} times, purl to last marker, sm; with A, work in K1, P1 Rib to end of row – 107{109, 117, 125, 133} sts.

Neckband

Row 1 (Decrease Row – RS): With A, work in K1, P1 Rib to first marker, remove marker; (k17{11, 10, 8, 7}, k2tog) 4{6, 8, 10, 12} times, knit to last marker, remove marker; work in K1, P1 Rib to end of row – 103{103, 109, 115, 121} sts.

Row 2: *P1, k1; rep from * to last st, p1.

Row 3: Knit the knit sts and purl the purl sts to end of row.

Rep Row 3 until neckband measures about 2½" (6.5 cm) from beg, end with a WS row as the last row you work.

Next Row (Buttonhole Row): K1, p1, k1, yo, k2tog, knit the knit sts and purl the purl sts to end of row.

Next Row: Knit the knit sts and purl the purl sts to last 5 sts, (p1, k1) twice, p1.

Rep Row 3 until neckband measures about 3" (7.5 cm) from beg, end with a RS row as the last row you work.

Bind off all sts in rib.

FINISHING

Sew Sleeve and underarm seams.
Sew buttons along left front, opposite buttonholes.
Weave in ends.

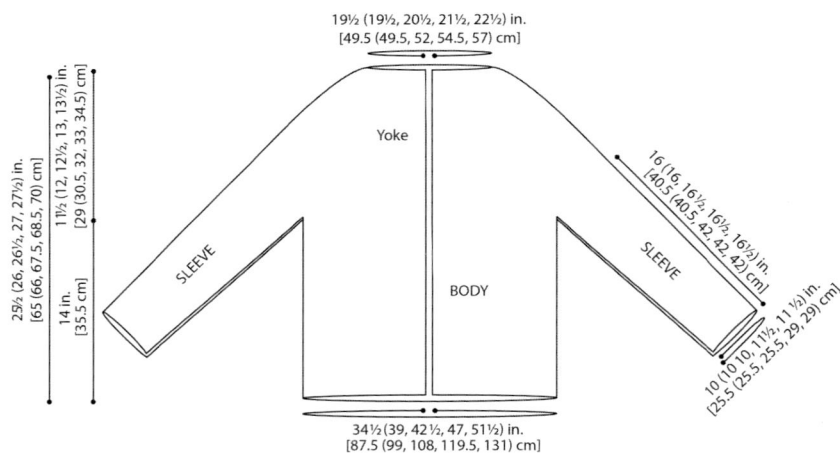

19½ (19½, 20½, 21½, 22½) in.
[49.5 (49.5, 52, 54.5, 57) cm]

25½ (26, 26½, 27, 27½) in.
[65 (66, 67.5, 68.5, 70) cm]

11½ (12, 12½, 13, 13½) in.
[29 (30.5, 32, 33, 34.5) cm]

14 in.
[35.5 cm]

Yoke

SLEEVE

BODY

SLEEVE

16 (16, 16½, 16½, 16½) in.
[40.5 (40.5, 42, 42, 42) cm]

10 (10, 10, 11½, 11½) in.
[25.5 (25.5, 25.5, 29, 29) cm]

34½ (39, 42½, 47, 51½) in.
[87.5 (99, 108, 119.5, 131) cm]

GENERAL INSTRUCTIONS

ABBREVIATIONS

beg = begin(ning)(s)
CDD = center double decrease
cm = centimeters
dpn = double-pointed needle(s)
k = knit
k2tog = knit 2 stitches together
M1L = make 1 left leaning
M1P= make 1 purl
M1R = make 1 right leaning
mm = millimeters
p = purl
pm = place marker
p2tog = purl 2 together
rem = remain(ing)(s)
rep = repeat
rnd(s) = round(s)
RS = right side
sm = slip marker
ssk = slip, slip, knit
st(s) = stitch(es)
St st = Stockinette stitch
w&t = wrap and turn
WS = wrong side
yo = yarn over

* — When you see an asterisk used within a pattern row, the symbol indicates that later you will be told to repeat a portion of the instruction. Most often the instructions will say, repeat from * so many times.

( ) or [ ] — Sets off a short number of stitches that are repeated or indicates additional information.

- When you see - (dash) followed by a number of stitches, this tells you how many stitches you will have at the end of a row or round.

GAUGE

Never underestimate the importance of gauge. Achieving the correct gauge assures that the finished size of your piece matches the finished size given in the pattern.

KNIT TERMINOLOGY	
UNITED STATES	INTERNATIONAL
gauge =	tension
bind off =	cast off
yarn over (YO) =	yarn forward (yfwd) **or**
	yarn around needle (yrn)

KNITTING NEEDLES		
UNITED STATES	ENGLISH U.K.	METRIC (mm)
0	13	2
1	12	2.25
2	11	2.75
3	10	3.25
4	9	3.5
5	8	3.75
6	7	4
7	6	4.5
8	5	5
9	4	5.5
10	3	6
10½	2	6.5
11	1	8
13	00	9
15	000	10
17	---	12.75
19	---	15
35	---	19
50	---	25

CHECKING YOUR GAUGE

Work a swatch that is at least 4" (10 cm) square. Use the suggested needle size and the number of stitches given. If your swatch is larger than 4" (10 cm), you need to work it again using smaller needles; if it is smaller than 4" (10 cm), try it with larger needles. This might require a swatch or two to get the exact gauge given in the pattern.

METRICS

As a handy reference, keep in mind that 1 ounce = approximately 28 grams and 1" = 2.5 centimeters.

TERMS

fasten off — To end your piece, you need to simply cut and pull the yarn through the last loop left on the needle. This keeps the last stitch intact and prevents the work from unraveling.

right side — Refers to the front of the piece.

Yarn Weight Symbol & Names	LACE 0	SUPER FINE 1	FINE 2	LIGHT 3	MEDIUM 4	BULKY 5	SUPER BULKY 6	JUMBO 7
Type of Yarns in Category	Fingering, size 10 crochet thread	Sock, Fingering, Baby	Sport, Baby	DK, Light Worsted	Worsted, Afghan, Aran	Chunky, Craft, Rug	Super Bulky, Roving	Jumbo, Roving
Crochet Gauge* Ranges in Single Crochet to 4" (10 cm)	32-42 sts**	21-32 sts	16-20 sts	12-17 sts	11-14 sts	8-11 sts	6-9 sts	5 sts and fewer
Advised Hook Size Range	Steel*** 6 to 8, Regular hook B-1	B-1 to E-4	E-4 to 7	7 to I-9	I-9 to K-10½	K-10½ to M/N-13	M/N-13 to Q	Q and larger

*GUIDELINES ONLY: The chart above reflects the most commonly used gauges and hook sizes for specific yarn categories.

** Lace weight yarns are usually crocheted with larger hooks to create lacy openwork patterns. Accordingly, a gauge range is difficult to determine. Always follow the gauge stated in your pattern.

*** Steel crochet hooks are sized differently from regular hooks–the higher the number, the smaller the hook, which is the reverse of regular hook sizing.

⬛⬜⬜⬜ BASIC	Projects using basic stitches. May include basic increases and decreases.
⬛⬛⬜⬜ EASY	Projects may include simple stitch patterns, color work, and/or shaping.
⬛⬛⬛⬜ INTERMEDIATE	Projects may include involved stitch patterns, color work, and/or shaping.
⬛⬛⬛⬛ COMPLEX	Projects may include complex stitch patterns, color work, and/or shaping using a variety of techniques and stitches simultaneously.